FILMING WITH ATTENBOROUGH

DONALD WOODS
FILMING WITH ATTENBOROUGH
THE MAKING OF
CRY FREEDOM

Foreword by
Sir Richard Attenborough

AN OWL BOOK
HENRY HOLT AND COMPANY
NEW YORK

For Charles and Camille Morgan

Published by Henry Holt and Company, Inc.,
521 Fifth Avenue, New York, New York 10175.
Published in Canada by Fitzhenry & Whiteside Limited,
195 Allstate Parkway, Markham, Ontario L3R 4T8.

LIBRARY OF CONGRESS CATALOGING-IN-PUBLICATION DATA
Woods, Donald, 1933–
Filming with Attenborough.
"An Owl book."
Also based on Woods's *Biko* (© 1978) and
Asking for trouble (1981).
1. Cry freedom. 2. Attenborough, Richard.
3. Biko, Stephen, 1946–1977, in motion pictures.
4. Woods, Donald, 1933–   , in motion pictures.
5. Political prisoners—South Africa—Biography.
6. Journalists—South Africa—Biography. 7. South
Africa—Race relations. I. Attenborough, Richard.
II. Woods, Donald, 1933–   . Biko. III. Woods,
Donald, 1933–   . Asking for trouble. IV. Cry
freedom. V. Title.
PN1997.C8853W6   1987   791.43′72   87-19675
ISBN 0-8050-0661-3 (pbk.)

First Edition

Designer: Beth Tondreau Design
Printed in the United States of America
1   3   5   7   9   10   8   6   4   2

ISBN 0-8050-0661-3

Contents

Photo sections follow pages 20, 52, 84, and 116.

Foreword by
Sir Richard Attenborough

I f I had met Donald Woods without knowing anything of his life, I doubt if I would have thought he possessed a more than passing share of heroism. Superficially, Donald is an amiable extrovert. I suspect that it would take a great deal to make him angry. He is not by any means an energetic person. Neither is he given to pontificating. Yet scratch the surface geniality, delve beneath the bon vivant, and you discover one of the most unlikely heroes of our time.

Donald is a white, fifth-generation, English-speaking South African. He comes from a society where white children absorb racism from the moment of their birth and where most of them grow up genuinely believing they are inherently superior to the black majority.

It is relatively easy for those of us born outside South Africa to condemn these attitudes. In my own case it required no leap of the imagination, since hatred of racism in all its forms was instilled from a very early age by my parents. But Donald Woods had no such role models on which to pattern his liberal beliefs. As a young man, in fact, he supported apartheid. It took a certain amount of bravery, as a mature adult, to admit he had been wrong. But the true nature of Donald's courage was not put to the test until he was in his forties, married, with five young children. This was when he met Steve Biko, whom he hailed publicly as the most impressive man he had encountered. For a white South African, paying such tribute to a black man fourteen years his junior was, in itself, a triumph of private enlightenment over a lifetime of public conditioning.

When Steve Biko died from beatings received in police detention in 1977, Donald Woods threw himself and the entire resources of his newspaper behind a campaign to force the authorities to hold an inquest. As a result he was declared a banned person, forbidden to be with more than one person at a time—other than members of his immediate family—confined to the magisterial district around his home, and prohibited from writing anything, even from keeping a diary. The ban was imposed for a period of five years.

With his income ensured, Donald could easily have sat out those five years in his luxurious South African home. Instead, he opted to evade constant police surveillance and escape abroad, leaving everything—house, savings, cars, relatives, and friends—to be free to proclaim the truth about Steve Biko's death and the atrocities of the apartheid system to the world.

He and his family came to England virtually penniless with only one suitcase of clothes and possessions among the seven of them. In my view that displays immense courage of a very high order indeed; one should not forget that Donald was joined in this decision by his steadfast and equally courageous wife, Wendy.

Most of us, if we are thinking, sensate people, have moral convictions of one kind or another. But how many, I wonder—myself included—would be prepared to sacrifice our entire lifestyle, all our creature comforts, for such a cause?

In this book Donald has written about making the film *Cry Freedom*. Like its author it is thoroughly entertaining; a good read from an involved outsider who records our antics as filmmakers with amusement and affection. I only hope that the film itself does full justice to Donald's courage and to that of his family—Wendy, Dillon, Jane, Duncan, Gavin, and Mary Woods.

—Richard Attenborough
London, England, May 1987

FILMING WITH ATTENBOROUGH

PROLOGUE

Despite being a lifelong optimist I couldn't quite believe the good news I was hearing in a telephone conversation with Sir Richard Attenborough. For a month he had deliberated whether or not to make a major film based on my writing, and now he was telling me his decision was yes.

That wasn't how he put it, exactly. The British tend not to say things that bluntly, and nobody I know is more British than Sir Richard. His actual words over the phone were: "Well, you know, I think I'd like to have a go at it."

Having by that time lived among the British for six years, I correctly interpreted this to mean: "My decision is a clear, emphatic, and positive yes!" And had I known him then as I was later to know him, I would have interpreted it further as: "What is more, *nothing* is going to stop me making this film—neither fire nor flood, nor principalities nor powers; neither the machinations of men nor the devices of demons."

1

He had taken a long time to think it over because he knew he'd be stepping into a political minefield of problems from the moment of commitment. The film would have many powerful enemies. Foremost among these, of course, would be the South African government, infuriated at the idea of a major antiapartheid production released worldwide.

Pretoria's propagandists already had their hands full trying to counteract the many television dramas and programs about apartheid circulating in the West, but here they were faced for the first time with the prospect of a big-budget feature film with the guarantee of mass audiences and global distribution. The apartheid system would be held up for general public inspection as never before.

When the South African government ordered a bombing raid in Zimbabwe shortly before we were scheduled to start filming on location I asked Attenborough if this event had diminished his enthusiasm; he replied with a bark of laughter: "You must be joking!" If anything, the bombing raid had increased his relish for the project.

Other powerful interests, including foreign corporations with holdings and investments in South Africa, were early opponents of the film. International big business didn't want an antiapartheid film, and, because of bank and business financing of American film studios, most of the major Hollywood honchos had been cool to the idea of the film before 1983. A movie's success on a big scale internationally is greatly assisted if backed by the massive distribution resources of one of the giant American studios—Universal, Paramount, Columbia, MGM, United Artists, Warner Bros., Disney, and 20th Century-Fox—and for years the subject of apartheid had been regarded by many key decision-makers in the investment and film communities as politically "too hot to handle" or "unbankable," therefore commercially untenable.

By 1983 we were helped by a remarkable old man in a loincloth—Mahatma Gandhi—in that the critical and commercial success of Attenborough's *Gandhi* showed that a political film on an issue remote from the awareness of the average American could nevertheless be a box-office winner. No wonder some of his friends recognized the Indian custom of adding *ji* onto names as a sign of affection, as in "Gandhiji," and referred to Attenborough on occasion as "Dickiji."

2

What also helped was Attenborough's track record as a maker of big movies. In *A Bridge Too Far* he had shown he could handle big-budget pictures with crowd scenes of De Mille proportions; in fact, the 400,000 extras in the *Gandhi* funeral scene had made the multitudes of Cecil B. look modest by comparison.

The success of *Gandhi* coincided with the belief of Frank Price, who had moved from Columbia to head Universal, that the time was right for a film on apartheid, and when his friend Attenborough proposed such a film, Price concurred. Nineteen eighty-three was clearly the year of Attenborough, and I was lucky that it was my work he chose to base his next production on. This finally came about because of a chance chat with a friend named Michael Stern; but the notion of ever being involved with a film began as a private joke, and a bitter one at that, on New Year's Eve of 1977. I was literally on the run from the South African Security Police, and had just dived face-first into the damp sand of a riverbank to evade a powerful police searchlight. As its beam swept over me I had two thoughts, one of which was: "Is this really happening to me?" The other was: "This is getting like a bloody film script!"

For what seemed a long time I lay motionless in abject fear after the beam had swept on, and concluded it must have been no more than a powerful car headlight. Later I learned it had indeed been a police searchlight, and that there had been a manhunt on that night— not for me, but for bank robbers who had shot a guard and headed for the Lesotho border near the village of Sterkspruit. This happened to be near the small border post of Telle Bridge which I had chosen because of its remoteness. My plans hadn't included an unscheduled bank robbery.

The searchlight scene doesn't appear in our film, Attenborough and scriptwriter John Briley regarding it as a film cliché. When you're telling a story through film you learn to leave out incidents, however true, that would be hard for audiences to accept. It was found, for example, after the release of *A Bridge Too Far* that audiences hadn't found Ryan O'Neal credible as a colonel—he didn't appear old enough—although the real-life colonel he had played had been two years younger than O'Neal. Factual reality doesn't always match cinematic credibility.

The problem of balancing cinematic credibility with factual truth was to engage us for more than two years before we began filming in Zimbabwe on July 14, 1986.

On the day we began filming in Harare I watched the cameras and lights and cables being set up and could hardly believe it was happening. I have been told that out of every one hundred manuscripts sent to American or British publishers, fewer than five are accepted for publication. Out of every one hundred books published, fewer than four are optioned for film rights, and out of every one hundred optioned fewer than three are actually made into films. This puts the odds against a book being made into a film at more than 22,000 to one. The odds are even higher against getting a producer-director of the caliber of Attenborough, backed by the biggest of all the major studios, Universal Pictures.

I had never seen a film being made before, and knew nothing of the techniques and complexities of the craft. I knew no more about films and filming than the average moviegoer, and it came as a surprise to find that the director actually said things like "Action!" and "Cut!"

As a journalist I had long known the inaccuracy of the image the general public had of newspaper offices, especially when it came to things like green eyeshades and shouts of: "Stop the presses! Hold the front page!" I had supposed that the film industry was subject to the same public misconceptions and romanticisms. Yet here was the canvas chair labeled DIRECTOR; there the caravans for the stars; you could hear the clack of the clapperboard and the camera call of the first assistant director: "Roll!"

It was all heady stuff for a former country boy from the South African backveld, and it seemed an appropriate moment to reflect on what had led up to that moment—in particular what had occurred since my wry observation on diving out of the beam of that searchlight.

How I came to be evading searchlights on the South African border was the subject of my book *Asking for Trouble*, and one of the ways in which I had asked for trouble was by writing my book *Biko*.

I was born in the Transkei Territory of South Africa in December 1933, and like most white South Africans had a highly conservative upbringing—especially on the subject of race. White minority privilege over the black majority in our country seemed the natural order of things, and my views on race only began to change when I left high school and was a law student in Cape Town, later traveling abroad to work as a journalist in Britain, Canada, and the United States.

I returned to South Africa in 1960 and five years later I was appointed editor-in-chief of the *Daily Dispatch* in the seaport city of East London. About ten years thereafter I met and became a friend of the dynamic young black leader Steve Biko, which intensified my opposition to the apartheid system of statutory racism. Before I knew him and came to understand his position fully, I had attacked him editorially for leading what had appeared to me then to be an extreme, too radical group known as BCM, the Black Consciousness Movement.

When Biko died violently in Security Police custody in September 1977 I was one of those who challenged, in my case through editorials and speeches, the official government claim that he had died of a hunger strike. On October 19 while en route to a speaking engagement in the United States I was arrested at the Johannesburg airport and banned— forbidden by the government to write, travel, speak publicly, or associate freely with other people for a five-year period.

During this period of virtual house-arrest, under surveillance, I decided to escape abroad with my family to publicize the Biko case and to help campaign for international pressures against the South African government. As part of this resolve I would take with me a manuscript I had written clandestinely while banned—a book about Steve Biko.

I was to travel in disguise, dressed as a priest and with my gray hair dyed black, to the Lesotho border, while my wife Wendy and our five children went there by another route. After a twelve-hour journey I reached the banks of the Telle River across which lay the independent black-ruled kingdom of Lesotho.

This was how I came to be dodging a police searchlight, thereby living through a film cliché too trite to be included in a real film . . .

1

VARIOUS OPTIONS

After getting across the border into Lesotho I was reunited with Wendy and the children in the capital, Maseru; we then flew via Botswana, Zambia, and Tunisia to London. There I delivered the manuscript of *Biko* to the publisher as arranged by a friend, and within a short while there were a number of approaches from producers in Britain and America who wanted to option the book for film rights.

It was while I was on a lecture tour of the United States that my publisher concluded an option deal with producer Carl Foreman, and during the next five years there were on-again-off-again attempts by Foreman to get one of the major studios interested in the movie. At various stages, MGM and later Columbia seemed on the point of agreeing, only for some event to nullify the campaign by Foreman and his partner, Ike Jones, a black producer who was particularly committed to the project.

In March 1979 one of the major studio chiefs actually shook hands on the deal with Foreman and Jones, and lawyers were drawing up the appropriate contracts when desperate pleas from the South African subsidiary company of the studio derailed the project. You see, economic sanctions do work. This setback, one of many, was a bitter disappointment to all of us. Ironically it was only after the option period on *Biko* had expired that Carl Foreman finally got Columbia interested enough to pursue the project. But there was a new snag—the studio would not allow me script approval. Wendy and I felt that if we lost control, commercial interests would intervene, jeopardizing the story's authenticity.

As it became known that the book was no longer under option, other producers began to seek the film rights—but none of them would guarantee adherence to *Biko*'s factual accuracy, and by 1983 it began to look as if there would be no film. Some aggressive producers threatened to go ahead anyway, claiming the Biko story was in the public domain. It seemed time to call for help from a special friend.

Alabama Rumpole

A man some people call "Rumpole U.S.A." in reference to John Mortimer's hero of litigation is Charles (Chuck) Morgan, Jr., formerly of Alabama, who with his wife, Camille, runs a formidable law firm in Washington, D.C. At one time head of the American Civil Liberties Union, he now directs a brigade of lawyers through the intricacies of the American legal system when not following the fortunes of the football team known throughout Alabama as the Crimson Tide. He wears braces, which the Americans call suspenders, and in his seersucker suit, with a lock of hair falling forward on his brow, he looks like a movie version of a southern yokel. It helps Morgan immensely when his legal opponents fall prey to this dangerous illusion.

Even more deceptive in image is his wife, Camille, whose southern drawl sounds at times like the melodious twang of a cello string and whose air of quiet domesticity masks a mind like a honed razor which I would back in discernment against the Lord Chief Justice of England.

Wendy and I had met Chuck and Camille back in 1972, when my newspaper celebrated its one hundredth anniversary and we wanted a distinguished guest speaker from abroad to address our centenary banquet. I had heard of his record as a civil rights lawyer in Alabama; how he had defied the Ku Klux Klan to get blacks registered and how he had become known as an orator against racism. I liked the idea that our centenary dinner audience, consisting inevitably of many conservative white newspaper editors and proprietors from all over South Africa, would be addressed by a white southerner castigating apartheid in the cadences of Dixieland.

Morgan was renowned for his wit, witness his comment when Governor George Wallace, barred by the Alabama constitution from succeeding himself as governor, installed his wife, Lurleen, in the state house to keep the gubernatorial seat warm for his return: "We have heard of politics makin' strange bedfellows," drawled Morgan, "but heah we have bedfellows makin' strange politics."

At our centenary banquet he had fulfilled our expectations with a memorable address which had visibly upset the digestion of his captive audience; they got the message that segregation was as doomed in South Africa as it had been in Alabama, and that the traditional arguments in its favor were as false in South Africa as they had been proved false in the American South.

I have been fortunate in having good lawyers as friends, people who have defended and represented me free of charge. In South Africa my former law tutor, Harold Levy, had twice kept me out of prison through skilled advocacy when the government tried to use statute law prosecution, and it was probably through frustration at having failed by this route that they eventually shut me up with a banning order that couldn't be challenged in court. In the United States Chuck Morgan had also represented me free of charge when I was setting up a scholarship and aid fund for black exiles from South Africa. Now I turned to him for protection against the Los Angeles lawyers representing the producers who threatened to do their own film version of *Biko*. Despite Morgan's brilliance, there was still no producer prepared to offer me script approval.

Enter Gandhiji

Around this time Attenborough's *Gandhi* exploded on the film world and scooped eight Oscars in the 1983 Academy Awards ceremony. While watching a television documentary on the making of *Gandhi* I thought what a pity it was that Attenborough hadn't been among the producers seeking the option on *Biko*. He was obviously a producer one could trust to preserve the integrity of the story. At the same time I realized he couldn't possibly consider it. Having done the story of a political martyr in a distant country, he would hardly want to follow up with the story of another political martyr in another distant country.

There was an inquiry about the film rights from a company called Chrysalis-Yellen around this time. They had just filmed for television the story of Jacobo Timerman, the Argentine editor, under Timerman's book title: *Prisoner Without a Name, Cell Without a Number*. I met and was impressed with the director of the film, Linda Yellen, and was seriously considering the Chrysalis-Yellen offer when I received a phone call from my friend Michael Stern.

Michael, founder of the first nonracial school in Southern Africa, Waterford-Kamhlaba in Swaziland, was a man of deep enthusiasms, and when he said "Richard Attenborough should make your film," I tried to hide my lack of interest as I replied: "Yes, but he won't!"

"Why not?" demanded Michael.

I gave him all the usual commercial reasons.

"Well, I happen to know he has long wanted to make an antiapartheid film," said Michael. Then I remembered that Michael was a friend of Attenborough's. The connection was the Waterford School, which Attenborough supported through financial donations and as chairman of its UK board of trustees. My interest grew as Michael added that Attenborough had read my book *Biko* when it was first published, but hadn't read *Asking for Trouble*.

"Send him a copy today!" said Michael. "He's leaving for China soon and will have time to read it while he's away. The two books together might make the basis of a film."

I thanked him for the suggestion and ended the call without intending to act on it for what now seem like absurd reasons. It sounded like Attenborough was too busy to read the book and I hated to make the effort to mail the thing at the time of day when I knew the post office would be crowded and unpleasant. Also, I had only one copy of the book in the house; it cost nine pounds, and it seemed certain that sending it to Attenborough would be tantamount to throwing it away

9

along with the nine quid. Besides, there was a television program starting that I very much wanted to see, so I settled down to watch it.

But then I began to think—even if it seemed a million-to-one chance, was it right to ignore the minuscule possibility? What if twenty years later one discovered that if Attenborough had read the book he would have decided to make the film?

Feeling somewhat foolish, I fetched the book and went through the long ritual of standing in line at the Surbiton post office to mail the package to the address Michael had given me.

Having thus placated the hobgoblins of chance, I put the matter out of mind as I pursued the prospects of the approach from Chrysalis-Yellen. A letter from Clare Howard, Attenborough's assistant, thanking me for the book and stating that Sir Richard would try to read it while away on his travels, seemed no reason for me to dwell on miraculous possibilities.

Shortly thereafter I met one of the most experienced filmmakers in Britain. Norman Spencer has impressive credits, having worked on *Lawrence of Arabia, The Bridge on the River Kwai, Great Expectations, Oliver Twist, The Sound Barrier, Brief Encounter*, and *Zorba the Greek*. He had worked closely with the legendary British director Sir David Lean, serving at different times as scriptwriter, assistant director, associate producer, and co-producer. Norman had produced his own picture, *Vanishing Point*, in the United States. He was to prove a walking reference book of information on the intricacies of the contemporary film industry.

I met Norman through a mutual acquaintance who wanted to explore the prospect of an independent production in the event that Chrysalis-Yellen might not offer a satisfactory deal, or that Attenborough might not be interested. Immediately interested in the subject of the film, Norman explained the various ways in which the project could be developed, and said that regardless of who might ultimately make the film the first requirement would be detailed research going beyond my own writing. His enthusiasm was infectious, though mine was dampened somewhat when he explained that my role would involve months of painstaking research and writing.

His perception—and that of every producer who had shown any interest—was that a film purely about Steve Biko would not succeed internationally; that the way to interest audiences in the Northern Hemisphere about the evils of apartheid would be to base the story line primarily on the friendship between Biko and me and on the events that befell us and our families during 1976 and 1977.

This meant chronicling every conceivable incident in the lives of Steve Biko and myself as well as contingent incidents in South Africa during that period which might be considered useful to a scriptwriter. I pointed out to Norman that this would amount to the equivalent of writing a thirty-hour film script, and was appalled when his phlegmatic response was to pull his veteran portable typewriter toward him and say: "That's right. Let's begin at the beginning."

For the next four months, working all day and often well into the night, with Norman driving all the way from Denham to Surbiton each morning, we kept at it until the monstrous work lay completed in two big volumes of typescript. Every word of it was typed by the imperturbable Norman on the deceptively fragile-looking portable which was later to accompany us on location all over Zimbabwe, to Mombasa in Kenya, and to Shepperton Studios back in London.

I had never met anyone as methodical and painstaking about detail. A compulsive enterer of times, dates, and developments into his diary, Norman chronicled every event, phone call, and inquiry about the project in his ubiquitous book of facts, and that is how I know it was precisely at 3:32 P.M. on August 26, 1983, that I heard by phone from Sir Richard that he was interested. He had some further traveling, reading, and research to do himself, after which he would propose a meeting for further discussion about the possibilities.

I did a quick caper around the kitchen table, where Norman was soldiering on at the typewriter working on some notes I had written the night before. He was also delighted at the news, but in a more restrained British way.

He and Attenborough had known each other for many years, and talked, I was later to find, the same kind of filmspeak, in which people like Charles Laughton, Charlton Heston, and Sir John Gielgud were referred to respectively as "Charley Laughton," "Chuck Heston," and "dear old Johnny G., bless him." I asked Norman what Attenborough was like as a person, and, having heard Prince Charles on television referring to Sir Richard as "Dickie," I was not surprised when Norman lapsed immediately into filmspeak. "Oh, Dickie's marvelous," he began. "You couldn't get anyone better, especially after *Gandhi* while he is what we in the industry call 'hot' . . . "

Sir Richard Live

Although I'd never met Attenborough I had the feeling moviegoers often get about famous actors—the feeling that you know them well through having seen them so often on the screen. All my life, it seemed, I'd been seeing him in a multitude of roles, beginning with the part of Percy Boone, the teenage thief, in *London Belongs To Me*, and most recently as the murderous major in *Conduct Unbecoming*. Attenborough was obviously unaware that he had been a constant visitor to the Colosseum, East London, South Africa, thus accompanying me through life amusing, terrifying, and moving me without even knowing me.

It was like what had happened many years ago to my old friend, Chaim Katz, a building contractor from East London who had always wanted to visit Israel. When Katz's business was firmly established he set forth on the great journey. It was before the age of long-distance jets and he had to proceed from East London through a series of flights via Johannesburg, Nairobi, and Entebbe. It was while waiting at Entebbe airport in Uganda for his next flight that he recognized a familiar face from home, so he went up and greeted the man warmly. The man looked puzzled, so Chaim said: "I'm Chaim Katz, the builder, and I know you from East London!" The man looked even more puzzled, so Chaim said: "I'm also from East London, like you! I see you often there!"

The man said: "East London?"

Chaim said: "Ya! East London, South Africa! Vere ve both come from!"

The man said he was sorry but he'd never been to East London, South Africa. He added that he was a film actor, and that his name was Stewart Granger.

"Oh! Oh!" said Chaim, clapping both hands to his cheeks in mortification. "The Colosseum!"

So as I prepared for my first meeting with Sir Richard Attenborough I knew him a lot better than he knew me.

Norman and I arrived at the Attenborough house on Richmond Green, a centuries-old former friary, to be greeted warmly by Sir Richard. It being real life, he was now in permanent Technicolor, and one had an immediate impression of pink-cheeked good health, white hair which seemed somehow more abundant than it actually was, and a youthful bounce which belied his sixty years. His features were animated and expressive and his movements vigorous. He looked full of energy—a dynamo of activity.

Over the next two years I was to realize the inadequacy of this description.

Lady Attenborough was as welcoming and friendly. I recalled having seen her in films, though she had long given up acting to give her full concentration to family life, and now spent some of her time serving as a magistrate. I later concluded that the atmosphere of affection in the close-knit Attenborough family must have resulted in many a clement magisterial decision for someone who had fallen foul of the law.

Sir Richard told us that he was interested in the idea of the film but it would arouse powerful opposition, and his description of the reprehensible capitalist interests that would resent it startled me—I had seen his olive-green Rolls-Royce Corniche parked beside Lady Attenborough's silver-gray Mercedes in the garage.

I should by now have been beyond being startled by the British, having the week before been driven, also by Rolls-Royce, to the Surrey country estate of the young multimillionaire socialist and spy novelist Ken Follett, who turned out best-selling thrillers as often as he campaigned for the Labour party to zap the rich with supertax. Other wealthy socialists I had recently met were Eric Woolfson, who churned out hit songs with easeful regularity, and Pete Townshend, formerly of The Who. It was interesting that they so strongly opposed Mrs. Thatcher's Conservative party—the only political party in Britain dedicated to keeping the very rich very rich.

Attenborough told Norman and me that he felt "a bloody good film" could be made on the basis of my books—provided a script with the right ingredients from both could be written. He thought that while *Biko* was the basic theme, *Asking for Trouble* provided "the way into" the movie, his reasoning being the same as Norman's—that the Woods story was the necessary balance to the Biko story if mass audiences

13

were to be reached in Europe and the United States. He added that, though he was "hugely attracted" to the idea, he needed time to look into all the implications of such a project, including the feasibility of finance and ultimate distribution, and he asked for a month for his deliberations.

I had been intrigued by the Attenborough manner of discourse. With precision of language, and pausing for as long as it took to find exactly the right word, he processed slowly from one corner of the room to the corner diagonally opposite, occasionally regarding the ceiling with intense interest as if looking for the elusive word there, which once found he would fling at you with a sudden concentrated stare of his bright eyes by way of emphasis. It was like being on the receiving end of two laser beams. Hands locked behind his back, with his feet angled out at ten to two, he would pace back and forth, back and forth in his diagonal gavotte, sometimes sweeping the air with an arm or grasping two fistfuls of space in a strangling motion as he thought out loud to us. Gusts of laughter would burst from him at an amusing thought, and occasionally he would stop pacing to stand behind a high-backed chair to use it as a kind of pulpit, thumping its top for emphasis or resting his forearms on it as he spoke.

My overall impression was of someone full of fun but thorough about what he took seriously, because even his occasional throwaway re-marks showed that a lot of thought and homework had gone into the subject under discussion. His precision of language included some ripe four-letter words about the South African government and its apartheid policy, but in general his speech was soft and in keeping with the ecclesiastic manner of his presentation.

A Twirler of Plates

Many months later when we were on location in Zimbabwe it was Norman who came up with the most accurate analogy of all for Atten-borough. We had been watching him vigorously directing scenes, then making use of the time taken for camera setups and lighting changes to rush off to the production office to hit the telephones to London, New York, Los Angeles, and wherever; and we talked of the non-cinematic Attenborough, wearer of many different hats.

He was variously chairman of Capital Radio, the Royal Academy of Dramatic Art, the British Film Institute, Goldcrest Films, the Actors Charitable Trust and Combined Theatrical Charities; a trustee of the Help a London Child Fund; president of the Muscular Dystrophy Group of Great Britain; Pro-Chancellor of Sussex University; board member of the Martin Luther King, Jr., Foundation; deputy chairman of TV Channel 4, of which he'd later become chairman; and chairman of U.K. Trustees of Waterford School in Swaziland.

I had wondered how he was able to juggle all these philanthropic balls while getting on with his business and professional life, and Norman had replied in his thoughtful way: "Dickie's not a juggler, really. He's more of a plate-twirler. You know the chap who spins a lot of plates on sticks, then while they're all spinning he stands in front and does card tricks until one of the plates behind him looks as if it's wobbling slowly enough to crash, then in the nick of time he rushes over to give it a twirl. That's how Dickie keeps all these things going— he's a plate twirler!"

After that first visit to the Attenborough home we had only a month to wait before finding out if our film was to be one of the plates to be twirled by the arch-twirler, and when the call finally came it was a memorable moment.

Testing the Water

Realizing by now the probability that I would be associated with him in this venture, I looked up some basic biographical details about Attenborough, including the brief notes in his book about the making of *Gandhi*. He had inherited his idealism from his parents, a couple who felt strongly about the dispossessed and persecuted. They had cared for Basque children who were refugees from the Spanish Civil War; distributed clothes to slum children, taking one with them every year on their summer holiday; and during World War II they adopted two young Jewish refugees from Nazi Germany. His legacy also included a lasting love of art and music and an affectionate family atmosphere which he and his wife of forty years shared in turn with their three children and grandchildren.

Drawn directly to the theater from school, Attenborough had had no doubts about which career he wanted, and, apart from war service in the Royal Air Force, acting was to be his life until he began to produce and direct. He starred in more than fifty films and plays, and he and his wife, Sheilashim, were in the original production of Agatha Christie's *The Mousetrap*, which was still packing in the crowds thirty-seven years later.

Attenborough had teamed up in 1958 with his friend Bryan Forbes to venture into filmmaking, since when all his major achievements in directing, producing, and acting contained an element of social comment. *The Angry Silence* was an indictment of the misuse of trade union power to ostracize a worker, a theme repeated in *I'm All Right, Jack!* though the latter was a satirical comedy. In *10 Rillington Place* the message was the horrors of capital punishment; in *Oh, What A Lovely War!* and *A Bridge Too Far* the horrors of war; and in *Gandhi* the moral power of nonviolence.

Attenborough saw our project as a potentially powerful indictment of apartheid as the worst example of racial persecution since Nazi Germany. It would also, as he conceived it, be an illustration of racial reconciliation between individuals as well as in a wider sense a plea for universal tolerance.

At our next meeting Attenborough said that if he could get the right financial commitments and a first-rate screenwriter our project could be formalized and contracts signed. The basis for the script would be my books and our two scenario tomes, and when Norman suggested we might edit the latter down for the convenience of the writer Attenborough opposed this. "Don't touch a word," he said. "Treat it as a rough cut— it's useful background and you never know what ideas it might produce."

Attenborough said his first choice as writer would be John Briley, who had won an Oscar for the screenplay of *Gandhi* and with whom he was already talking about our project. The question was whether Briley, who was in considerable demand after his Academy Award, would be available in view of his already heavy commitments. (In the end it was several months before Briley could even look at our project, yet Attenborough's regard for his writing was so high that he counted the delay worth it.) "We really must get Jack Briley if we can, my dears," he said. "He's a difficult bugger, a bit of a prima donna—but the bastard's brilliant!"

He added, a trifle glumly, that Briley would be "bloody expensive" in view of his Oscar, but brightened immediately on describing the latter's ability not only to construct an indispensable dramatic line but also to write taut dialogue and to compress profound thoughts into a few words. There had, for example, been a call from the White House, whose speechwriter had wanted to use the Gandhi quote "Poverty is the worst form of violence," only to learn that the quote was not that of Gandhiji but that of Brileyji.

Finance for the film did not seem to worry Attenborough much. His friend Jake Eberts, a Canadian who had started Goldcrest Films and had masterminded the financing of *Gandhi*, was ready and able to raise what was required; and another friend, Frank Price, who at Columbia had headed the distribution deal for *Gandhi*, was now with Universal and favored our project. Attenborough had obviously been testing the water while making up his mind.

When Jack Briley was finally free to be signed aboard, Wendy and I were invited to meet him to discuss his approach to the screenplay. We met him at the British Film and Television Academy in Piccadilly. A slim man with a boyish grin, he was easy to get along with socially, and for more than a year we met in various places and ate, drank, and laughed a good deal. We developed a real affection for him the more we got to know him. We also agreed that he was one of the most infuriating individuals we'd ever met.

He read and researched and thought so much about Steve Biko that he seemed to become convinced he knew Biko's attitudes better than we did. Certainly his exposition of Biko's stance through dialogue, condensed conversationally, was frequently masterful.

He had also read about and had visited South Africa, and was convinced, it seemed, that he knew our own country better than we did. It was especially galling to discover that he was occasionally right.

An American from Michigan, Jack had lived in London for many years but was now living and working abroad, so our working meetings had to be either in Paris or near Grasse in the south of France, where the Attenboroughs had an old Provençal farmhouse.

The contracts were signed in January 1984. They were drawn up by Claude Fielding, Attenborough's longtime friend and legal adviser, who looked and spoke exactly as if sent around by Central Casting—British Lawyer Type. Details of the contract were processed by Fielding, but most of it Attenborough and I agreed upon in a remarkably short time—compared with all the hassle that had gone on in previous negotiations with producers. When I first explained the worries Wendy and I had about losing control of the factual story he was unequivocal in his assurance: "Not one word will go into this film unless you are both satisfied it is true." This arrangement was his preference, because he felt the power of the story lay in its truth, and he wanted not only our constant scrutiny of the script as it evolved, but that of Steve Biko's other friends and relatives (to whatever extent this would be possible in view of the political situation in South Africa).

On the matter of script approval his word was enough guarantee for us, and it is a measure of the subtlety of the British ethos that, when an American friend was amazed we hadn't insisted on tying Attenborough up contractually on every detail of this understanding, it was difficult to explain that we regarded his oral promise more binding than any contract. In London a whispered remark at the bar of the Garrick is often worse censure than a lawsuit, there being no more pitiable creature among his peers than an English gentleman known to have broken his word.

Attenborough kept his word. Throughout the making of the film Wendy and I, or at least one of us, watched the shooting of every scene and saw the daily rushes, and though there were occasional disputes—often between ourselves—as to how upcoming scenes should be approached, nothing in the film was included without our concurrence.

Sometimes Attenborough disagreed with us and managed to convince us we were wrong on a point, but we were never summarily overruled or ignored if we dug in our heels. At such times he would suspend shooting to talk the matter out, taking pains to persuade us and in each case proceeding only when we were convinced. But these few instances were never matters of factual truth or political accuracy—he followed our judgment trustingly in those—but rather matters of what he felt worked best artistically.

Considering his gifts of persuasion, amounting sometimes to exquisite heights of manipulative deviousness, we were conscious throughout the production period of his adherence to the promise that we could police the entire process to our satisfaction. This was uppermost in my mind on the November day in 1986 when we finished shooting the last scene. We were full of emotion, and I enveloped him in a hug.

Getting to hug Attenborough was no light achievement—he usually got the hug in first. Uncharacteristically for someone so English, he proved a most demonstrative man. A prodigious kisser of practically every woman within reach at various times of day, he was also a shoulder-patter, arm-stroker, and hugger of all his associates—male or female. To see the hulking David Tomblin, his first assistant director, getting the shoulder pat and the arm stroke as they conferred before shooting a scene was like seeing a large sheepdog being readied by his trainer for a competitive performance.

Attenborough's affection was expressed verbally as well as physically. He called practically everyone "darling," with occasional variations such as "poppet" or "my love." The macho Briley was frequently addressed as "Jack, poppet" or "Jacko, darling," usually when Attenborough was about to launch a circuitous attack on one of Briley's pet intransigences.

On one occasion a burly studio worker resembling a rugby football player growled the question as to whether Sir Richard wanted a large table moved on the set, and Sir Richard, not hearing the question clearly, turned an ear toward him and breathed: "What's that, my heart?" Knowing the ways of "Sir" the burly one didn't blink an eye but merely repeated the question.

"Sir" was what the senior members of his production team called him, often in the third person when he wasn't present: "Have you asked Sir about this?" It was not obsequiousness, because the same people also called him, whether to his face or behind his back, "Dickie" or "Dick" or "Richard." One junior member of the unit called him "Biggus Dickus."

The opposite of pompous, Attenborough never talked down to anyone or pulled rank other than professionally among members of the unit, and never complained when anyone sat in his director's chair—although part of the reason might have been that he seldom gave himself time to sit down anywhere.

During the third week's shooting on location in Zimbabwe he became ill and was resting between camera setups in a small room on the set of a rural clinic when the carpenters constructing a platform for the camera started hammering loudly right by his window. One of the cast pointed out to the cockney carpenter that he was waking Sir Richard, which drew the reply: "Does 'e want to fuckin' sleep or does 'e want to make a fuckin' film!"

Amused at this succinct summary of the choices open to him, Attenborough emerged to pursue the latter option.

Biko in 1977—taken by an American photographer who worked for the *Daily Dispatch*.

Juanita Waterman and
Denzel Washington as
Ntsiki and Steve Biko.

Opposite, top, Donald
Woods and Kevin
Kline. Kline's hair
has been grayed.

*Opposite, bottom
left,* Donald and
Wendy Woods.

*Opposite, bottom
right,* Penelope Wilton
and Kevin Kline as
Wendy and Donald
Woods.

The real Woods family *(back row, left to right)*: Jane, Wendy, Dillon, Duncan, Gavin, Mary, and Donald. The screen Woods family *(left to right)*: Kate Hardie, Penelope Wilton, Graeme Taylor Adam, Hamish Stuart-Walker, Adam Stuart-Walker, Kevin Kline, with the youngest, Spring Stuart-Walker, on director Attenborough's lap.

Wendy Woods *(left)* with Penelope Wilton, who plays Wendy in the movie.

Jane Woods *(left)* and Kate Hardie, who plays Jane in the movie.

Sophie Mgcina, who plays the Woods's maid Evalina, with the actors playing the Woods children and a Zimbabwe dog as the Woods's dog, Charlie.

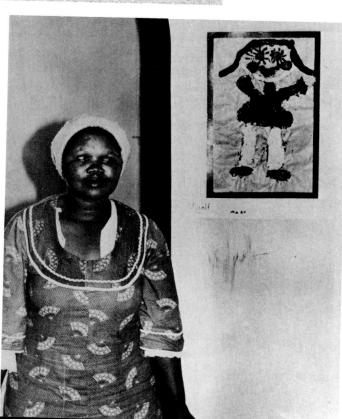

The real Evalina Mvunelwa.

The real Woods children, nine years older, on the porch of a replica of their South African house: *(standing)* Gavin, Dillon, and Mary; *(seated)* Jane and Duncan.

Another view of the house as constructed on a vacant lot in Harare, Zimbabwe. The hammer and sickle on the wall in the foreground was spray-painted on the original wall of the Woods's house in South Africa by Lieutenant Gerhard Cilliers of the Security Police, after which five bullets were fired at the house by his companion, Sergeant Johan Jooste.

2
THE PEOPLE

Shortly before making up his mind to go ahead with the film, Attenborough had felt it was important to go to South Africa. He had never been there and wanted to get the feel of the place, in particular to meet Steve Biko's widow and ask if she would favor the idea of a film involving the story of Steve. Another strong reason for the visit was his wish to meet some Gandhi relatives he hadn't yet met and to see places of Gandhian interest from the Mahatma's South African period. He also wanted to meet former Biko associates and other persons significant in black liberation politics in South Africa, and asked Wendy and me to write down the names of people we felt he should meet.

We wrote down a long list, realizing he could hardly get around to meeting even half of them on account of sheer logistics. In fact he met everyone on the list, as well as a few more—sometimes with the Security Police openly following.

21

Sir Richard and Lady Attenborough had a hectic tour in South Africa and their visit ended in a blaze of controversy, but their mission was accomplished and the highlights were visits to Steve Biko's mother and his widow Ntsiki, who thanked them for showing respect by consulting them and favored the film project with only one proviso: "Make it strong!" They also visited Biko's former associates, Dr. Mamphela Ramphele and Peter Jones, and other important political personalities including Winnie Mandela.

Toward the end of their visit, shortly after meeting with Winnie Mandela, the Attenboroughs had a taste of South African governmental smear tactics. Some official in Pretoria obviously decided it was time to discredit them, and the word was passed on to the government-controlled media. There followed an orchestrated distortion, especially on South African television, of Sir Richard's discussion with Winnie Mandela, and the evening news included a "news report" which was largely a fabrication.

Possibly the "reporter" (more likely a Security Policeman under cover as a reporter) listening near the door of Mrs. Mandela heard Sir Richard talking about "when shooting begins"—in reference to shooting the film—but as usual the South African viewers saw and heard only what their government wanted them to see and hear, namely that Attenborough planned to release a film to coincide with violence planned by the African National Congress.

This was the first of many ludicrous reports about our project over the next few years. They were to grow more vicious and more sophisticated as the project progressed, but we had expected this to happen. As with the more serious attacks later, this initial incident merely had the effect of making Attenborough more determined to go ahead with the film and to "make it strong." My own reaction to the news distortion was predominantly gratitude to the South African Broadcasting commissars for helping to nudge Attenborough into an extra gear of commitment to getting started on the film soon.

As with most film scripts, Briley's went through a number of drafts, each one better than the last, and for us one of the most enjoyable periods during the preproduction stage was the series of script conferences we had at the Attenborough farmhouse in the south of France.

Somewhere in France

The Attenboroughs had bought the old stone house many years before and had totally renovated it. It had a fine view from the broad terrace of the hills running down to the Mediterranean, and the whole of the top floor, the third level, was Attenborough's study.

I thought it the most pleasant room I had been in. Big, with window views on three sides, it had comfortable chairs and settees and window seats, with rugs on the floor and a corner fireplace. In another corner stood Attenborough's desk, with stereo equipment close at hand so that Mozart and Beethoven could keep him company as he plied the phones to London, New York, and Los Angeles. It was in this room that much friendly creativity, as well as abrasive disputation at times approaching unarmed combat, took place between Wendy and me on one side and Jack Briley on the other, with Norman Spencer in avuncular attendance and Attenborough refereeing, Sheila being at hand to mop up the metaphorical blood.

We would begin the work sessions after breakfast, Sheila disappearing occasionally to make tea or lunch, then in the evenings the Attenboroughs would take us to a restaurant in some neighboring village, of which there seemed an inexhaustible supply. France being the indisputable home of good food as an art form, it was a kind of gastronomic pilgrimage. The Attenboroughs were well acquainted with the various proprietors, who would greet them extravagantly, exchanging kisses on both cheeks and dramatic exclamations of goodwill.

Sheila spoke good French and Dickie not much, though you would never have guessed it to watch him in full Gallic cry. His shoulders and arms would become French, and he would supplement his basic vocabulary with an assortment of French-sounding groans through constricted throat muscles.

Wendy and I had in the others four prime sources for stories of the film trade, Jack Briley being as good a raconteur from his side of the industry as Sheila, Dickie, and Norman were from theirs. The script was seldom mentioned during these social evenings, or at least not the disputatious parts of it, which though not numerous were less than extremely rare.

Once or twice back in the Attenborough workroom the atmosphere became heated and Dickie had to intervene. Generally he stayed out of it and would let us argue on, speaking only after the verbal storm had peaked, when he would present a summing-up of the argument on both sides.

It was only after three days that I realized the full extent of Attenborough's talent for subtle manipulation and diplomatic deviousness. He could, through an apparently impartial statement of the opposing sides, arrive at the perfect compromise—which would, one suspected finally, be the answer he had decided on from the beginning. Those pauses while he appeared to grope for the right word, those pacings while he puzzled the point out in front of us, those rhetorical inquiries of the neutral air—many were spontaneous. But not all. Nor were all his reactions to our contention.

On one occasion when Jack and I were actually on our feet hurling angry words at each other Attenborough blew his top, slamming his script down and bellowing: "Stop this! You're behaving like children!" So loud was his shout, so dreadful his expression of outrage, that Jack and I were cowed into shamed silence. Only later came the realization that we'd been zapped with scene 22 of *Guns at Batasi* or some such tirade from the Attenborough repertoire. But it worked, and the compromise formula with which he followed this shock treatment was acceptable to all.

Once a point was resolved we would be back to our banter without lasting tension, because Attenborough could dissipate tension as well with a joke as with a bellow from Batasi. But that period at Grasse was more fun than fury because there was a high degree of consensus about Jack's script. Most of the contention was over how to interpret Steve Biko's essential political credo.

Initially we felt that Jack was making too much of Biko's statements that his movement had a policy of nonviolence, and that this was being projected into a principle of Biko's rather than a strategy of action for that time and in those circumstances in South Africa. Biko had never condemned violence as a matter of principle, and had in fact worked for the unification of the African National Congress and the Pan Africanist Congress, which were both committed to armed struggle. The nonviolent stance of the Black Consciousness Movement was a tactical recognition of the need for a movement within the country to function aboveground while the consciousness of blacks could be raised, and Biko and his associates emphasized this in order to prevent or delay the banning of the organization.

The more Jack quoted us passages from Biko's own words on the subject, the more we pointed out the circumstances and context of these quotations—under cross-examination in court, or to foreign journalists or other visitors whose reports might be the basis of prosecution against him. Ultimately we agreed on a formula proposed by Attenborough in which it was obvious from the script that Biko was essentially a peace-loving man who worked for a South African solution which ideally would preclude violence, but that he wasn't a pacifist who ruled out armed struggle under all circumstances and that he was, in fact, in the mainstream of black resistance, which recognized the role and options of the ANC and PAC and regarded their leaders as national heroes in the fight against apartheid.

Attenborough was entertaining in his enacted visualizations of how he considered certain scenes could be shot. He would act out several roles and even supply sound effects. On one occasion he became two Jeeps—complete with engine noises—and on another an elevator containing several Security Policemen, complete with nasty faces. This enthusiasm carried over into filming on location when, if there were off-camera sounds to be simulated for later dubbing, these noises would come from Attenborough himself. He was, at various times, a barking dog, a telephone ringing, a gun being fired, and a child screaming. When David Tomblin offered to get someone else to simulate the screaming child to save the Attenborough larynx, Sir Richard dug his heels in. "Not on your life—I *like* doing it!"

The Screenplay

The sessions in the south of France paid off, and when Jack's final draft emerged it looked a winner. Testing his ideas against our questions had strengthened his belief in most of them, while others had been developed further in his mind following our discussions, as we'd been able to supply information he needed for this final process.

Among the things we learned from the exercise was the complexity of the screenwriter's craft. Judging a script from the words on the page was like judging someone's build from a photograph of his skeleton. Unless you could visualize the totality of concepts in the script you couldn't appraise it, and its interlocking parts had to be interdependent so that the dramatic sweep of the whole was maintained without any weakness in any part. Norman Spencer described Jack's craft as akin to that of the watchmaker, ensuring that all the little working parts were integral to the whole mechanism.

What seemed daunting was that nobody could be certain until a film was finally edited whether the whole thing "worked" as an integrated theme, and filmmakers had to rely on guesswork and experience to judge before gambling millions on production. There could be general agreement that the script was excellent; that the actors gave a wonderful performance; that the daily rushes were impressive; but only the final edited version complete with soundtrack could reveal whether all this resulted in an excellent film.

To boil down into about two and a half hours a story covering several years of real life and real events—that was the essence of the script-writer's craft, and the script Jack Briley evolved produced a taut story line which covered the basic facts. Concentrating on real events in South Africa in 1976 and 1977, Briley used general incidents and developments as the "background" and particular incidents involving the Biko and Woods families as the "foreground" of the screenplay. My meeting with Steve Biko after I had attacked him in editorials; my "conversion" from the conventional white attitude and our developing friendship; the resentment of this by the Security Police; the sense of a net closing in on both families; the killing of Biko and our escape with the manuscript about the killing—these events were related through scenes based on fact. Fleshed out with Briley's dialogue and dramatic shape to the whole narrative, the script told a story of apartheid and South Africa as it had not been told before on the cinema screen, and even amateurs like Wendy and me could see the power of the story which Attenborough could now prepare to translate into film.

With the script completed, the next step for Attenborough was to assemble the unit, prepare a shooting schedule and budget, pick the actors, and decide where to make the film.

Assembling the Unit

To start putting the unit together Attenborough turned to his longtime associate, Terry Clegg, who had been in charge of production on *Gandhi*. Between the two of them they picked the main elements of the team. With Attenborough as producer and director, Terry Clegg as executive producer, and Norman Spencer and Jack Briley as co-producers, the assistant directors were headed by Attenborough's favorite first assistant director, David Tomblin. "The best in the world, as far as I am concerned," he said of Tomblin.

Terry Clegg, fresh from the Academy Award triumph of *Out of Africa*, on which he had been co-producer, had come up from the bottom of the film industry. Many of his "apprenticeship" chores had been on films in which Attenborough was lead actor. He had started as a mail runner at Pinewood Studios, then had become successively production runner; third assistant, second assistant, first assistant, location manager, unit manager, production manager, associate producer, and finally, executive producer. I asked him what he did first on being approached to do a film. "Read the script," he said. Clegg, a man of few words, had no time for "rubbish" and cared deeply about the caliber of the project he was going to spend a year or more of his life on.

On this project he and Attenborough were pleased to get a 95-percent first-choice rate of the crew they wanted, and inevitably these included many from the *Gandhi* crew.

After considering various African countries as locations to shoot the film in, Attenborough and Clegg had decided on Zimbabwe because of its nearness to South Africa and the consequent similarity of its countryside, vegetation, and people, though there was an element of risk in filming so close to the enemy. Clegg had an affinity for locations with the extra quality of proximity to good golf courses, and he had no complaints on this score about Zimbabwe. Harare alone had no fewer than twelve courses.

A ruminative man, he would watch the filming with his arms folded and his feet planted wide, and you never knew from his expressionless demeanor whether he was planning his next production or his next round of golf. He was later to display rare organizational skills when the crew was stranded without a flight out of Mombasa.

I asked him when he was prebudgeting whether it wouldn't be tempting to overbudget in order to look good later for staying within budget, and he replied: "You can't do that. You're working with professionals and reporting to experts, and if you played that sort of game you wouldn't get any more offers." The budget for our film was $22 million plus Universal's overhead of some $3 million; Universal might later spend between $10 and $15 million on promotion, so that the final cost could ultimately be over $35 million.

Clegg had been the first to approach the Zimbabwean government for fiscal approval of private Zimbabwean co-financing and for official cooperation during location shooting, and the Zimbabweans ultimately decided to do the internal co-financing governmentally. After several trips there by Jake Eberts this participation was finally settled on at around 7.5 million Zimbabwe dollars, roughly the equivalent of 4.5 million American dollars. This gave Zimbabwe a chance to earn foreign-currency profits and to gain training for its budding filmmakers and credit as a country to shoot films in. Ours was to be the fourth to be shot there within two years.

David Tomblin, first assistant director, was a hulking figure of a man in his mid-fifties. He appeared to have no neck, his head resting on massive shoulders as if he wore American football padding. He spoke in a low rumbling growl, barely moving his lips, and this ventriloquistic effect was often to be observed as he issued orders by walkie-talkie to his sidekicks, second assistant directors Roy Button and Patrick Kinney.

Tomblin didn't always resort to words. On one occasion when the background traffic action hadn't been choreographed as he had instructed Patrick Kinney to do it, he brought his large paw down on Patrick's head. The latter, needing no further communication, sped off to put the matter right.

When one of the actresses, Josette Simon, appeared on the scene, everyone admired her long slender neck. Attenborough said: "Josette has so much neck and David Tomblin so little—they ought to come to some sort of arrangement."

Beneath his gruff manner Tomblin is a kindly man. He was the first to consider the well-being of the children and animals involved in some of the filming, and as a successful writer for television he had a quick wit. When an actor mistook the cue word "Pots!" for the shout of "Stop!" he rumbled quietly to no one in particular: "Well, it *is* an anagram."

His specialty was background action, those seemingly unrelated movements in the background of a scene which the director orders and which we cinemagoers take for granted as somehow just happening. In a Tomblin street scene the casual passerby or jostling group on the sidewalk had the required movements designed precisely by him. Not just people, either. When Attenborough required a flock of pigeons to fly up suddenly out of the grass, a herd of cattle to wander in the distance, and even a gaggle of goats to block a rural road, these had to obey the Tomblin will in the matter of style and timing. Thus from time to time when watching the rushes or viewing a take we would hear the familiar growl: "Start the cattle moving!" or "Pigeons now!"

Later he was even to command the start and cessation of rain, and it was possibly because of his power to control the elements that he was not always a contented man on the golf course. If he hit a booming drive down the middle of the fairway he would rumble: "All very well, but my iron shots are off." If he hit a good iron shot he'd growl: "Pity I can't chip today . . . " His quest for excellence was unceasing, and when the ball dared to disobey his will you sensed him looking around for Roy and Patrick to put things right.

Roy Button and Patrick Kinney were, in Norman Spencer's opinion, the ideal second assistants, and he predicted both would go far in films. "Watch their eyes," he said. "Roy and Patrick are always on the lookout for what needs to be done, and that's what a good second assistant is for—to make everything go smoothly for the first assistant and therefore for the director."

David Tomblin's opposite number representing the Zimbabwe part of the team as co–first assistant director was Steve Chigorimbo, who though still in his mid-thirties had worked on a number of films in various capacities. But never one like this, he said, adding that he was learning more on this one than all the others put together. It was a question of expertise combined with attention to detail. He was watching at close quarters the Attenborough-Clegg-Tomblin interrelationship, and rated Terry Clegg as the best administrator he had worked under.

A tall, pleasant-featured man with a good sense of humor underlying strongly held political convictions, Steve Chigorimbo had played a key intelligence role for the Mugabe forces in the war against white minority rule, and was enthusiastic about Zimbabwe's drive to develop its film industry. Fluent in English, Shona, and SiNdebele, he was of crucial importance in the big scenes involving up to eighteen thousand extras, and his cries over the megaphone of "*Nyararai!*" ("Quiet!") and "*Mirai!*" ("Stand still!") were to become familiar during our three-month stay in Zimbabwe. They were even exported back to Shepperton by Patrick Kinney, for use against restless elements during the studio shooting.

Chigorimbo had some interesting comments about the script. As a black activist he had had initial reservations about a white-oriented film on apartheid, but once he read the script he saw it as the strongest possible cinematic indictment of apartheid in the international context—precisely because of its orientation. "Nobody who sees this film will be able to claim again that they don't know about apartheid!" he said. "They won't be able to claim it is not based on true facts . . . it's going to hit them hard!"

Preliminary scouting was done by Attenborough, Clegg, production chief accountant John Trehy, director of cinematography Ronnie Taylor, and production designer Stuart Craig. This was crucial to the entire operation, determining whether Zimbabwe was to be the location and for what reasons. There were many considerations: Could Stuart match the buildings in Harare to buildings in South Africa? Could sets be constructed better here than elsewhere? John Trehy, holding the money bags, had to work out budgets and minibudgets and compare costs; Ronnie had to devise camera concepts and angles with Attenborough. Many proposed locations in various parts of Zimbabwe had to be inspected. It was a long and exhaustive procedure.

At this stage it was in the experienced hands of these first members appointed to the unit by Attenborough and Clegg. Most of the other members I would get to know when shooting got under way in Zimbabwe.

Politics and Publicity

Attenborough's director of publicity, Diana Hawkins, kept an eagle eye out for premature leaks about the film and maintained close liaison with the publicity officials at Universal on all matters pertaining to public coverage of the project. This involved diplomacy and close knowledge of advantageous types of coverage—how to hold back the best publicity until around the film's release, while being reasonable about early coverage on a sparing and selective basis. It also involved ability to be wide awake in milliseconds if the wrong story broke late at night, and required skill in damage containment.

Fortunately Diana had had the experience on *Gandhi* of a highly controversial project, and as India had even more factions among its hundreds of millions of citizens than South Africa with its paltry thirty-three million, this one was not quite as taxing. But it had its own problems, because Attenborough and I were wide open to attacks not only from the white right but from the black left as well, for opposite reasons. The whites objected to our making an antiapartheid film they knew would hurt the South African government, and the radical blacks objected because they thought we soft white liberals would neither hit hard enough nor adhere to their preferred ideological line.

The small but militant rump of what had once been Biko's Black Consciousness Movement objected in principle to whites making a film about the leader they claimed as theirs alone, and the South African government media tried, ironically, to feed the flame of radical black resentment by implying that Attenborough and I were exploiting Biko's name purely for financial gain. Diana Hawkins fielded these attacks, replied to those that seemed worth replying to, and went for the low profile on the others.

Our feeling generally was that we should be judged on the film when it was released, and that it was pointless to get embroiled in controversy with persons who hadn't even seen the script. In this regard Attenborough had touched all the right bases politically, and had gone to Lusaka, Zambia, to consult the leadership of the African National Congress, showing them the script and talking it through with them, and receiving in return not only their blessing for the film but much practical help by way of suggestions from ANC members who had known Biko well.

He and I had also met leading members of the Pan Africanist Congress and had gained their endorsement for the project as well, since the PAC leadership took the same view as the ANC leadership—that

31

this film would inform the world about the evils of apartheid as no purely documentary film could.

Having covered the ANC and PAC concerns, and having consulted Biko's widow, mother, and associates in South Africa, we thought we had completed our preproduction inquiries of those who most mattered, but later we were to encounter problems from a quarter least expected.

Through all these developments Diana Hawkins was in close attendance, and it was clear that Attenborough relied heavily on her judgment not only about public statements and replies to queries about the film but on a wide range of general matters. As a problem came to mind he would turn from his position at the camera and look around for her, sometimes prefacing his question in moments of levity by calling her by her previous surname. "Carter, darling . . . ," he would begin, and in time I formed the impression that if Sir Richard were ever confronted at the pearly gates by Saint Peter with a range of awkward questions he would turn around and call: "Carter, darling . . . "

The Casting Coach

The final consideration, now that the script was completed, the production offices opened, and the budget planned, was the casting. Preliminary work had been done in this direction, but the cast had now to be firmed up because the preproduction period was drawing to a close and we had to be ready to start shooting in Zimbabwe in mid-July of 1986. The script called for a big cast, and we had less than six weeks left to complete it.

It was at this time that I met the extraordinary character Attenborough had chosen to be our casting director. Her name was Susie Figgis, and she had been casting director on *Gandhi* as well.

I was flying out by Air Zimbabwe to join Attenborough, Clegg, Norman Spencer, and others on a reconnaissance visit to various projected locations such as Harare, Gweru, Shurugwi, Bulawayo, Mutare, and Beira in Mozambique; the first leg of the flight was from Gatwick to Frankfurt, Germany. We were kept on board at Frankfurt while new passengers boarded for Harare, and I noticed what I took to be a German student coming aboard. I wondered if she was going out to work on a thesis. She looked a bit hippyish in her clothing and makeup, and I use the word "clothing" loosely—she had on little more than a very long and somewhat shabby T-shirt. Her dark hair was all over the place and she had two enormous eyes that stared hypnotically about her.

She leaned over to speak to me and I, flattered that this attractive young lady would pass the time of day, hastily prepared in my mind the small stock of two or three German phrases that comprise my entire Hanseatic vocabulary. Instead came this very English accent: "Are you Donald Woods?"

Good heavens, it was Susie Figgis . . .

It is always a mistake to form preconceived notions of people, but the name Susie Figgis had suggested to me the image of a middle-aged bespectacled lady in rather formal clothes and with the severe manner of a Margaret Thatcher. The real Susie Figgis couldn't be more different.

Born in Nairobi, Susie was brought to England by her parents when she was about ten, but managed to get expelled from a succession of schools and led a fairly aimless life until she discovered her skill as a casting director. She is unorthodox, doesn't keep files, and lies in bed for three nights thinking: "Shit, I can't think of anybody." Then, when she has managed to scare herself, ideas flood into her head and she completes the casting. Having done that, she flies off to Guatemala where she looks after abandoned children.

Why Guatemala?

"Why not?"

She had come across the problem of street children in Guatemala while working on a film project, and now collected money for them. She also employed people she paid more than herself, and was more unconscious about money than anyone I'd met.

How she managed to find such remarkable lookalikes for some of our key roles, as for the part of Ntsiki Biko, she ascribed to luck, because her choice of Juanita Waterman for the part was based on Juanita's acting more than her looks. It had to be, because she hadn't yet seen a picture of Ntsiki at that stage. . . . She judged Ntsiki's character by what she had read about her. John Matshikiza as Mapetla Mohapi and Josette Simon as Mamphela Ramphele were instant choices for her. She had felt certitude about 90 percent of the cast from the beginning.

33

The casting director's job, I learned, was to provide a pool of available actors for the director to choose from and to make recommendations about the order and suitability of those available.

The Major Roles

The part of Steve Biko had been the greatest problem. Here was the dominant influence in our story, so he had to be physically right and he had to have the charismatic presence of someone who had had such a powerful effect on people's lives. Ideally, he had to be a black South African.

Susie combed the earth for such an actor. She started in South Africa, looking at every leading actor of the appropriate age and size and looks, and although she came up with several who were physically right for the part, none of them showed enough acting skill at reading the scripted lines.

She looked beyond South Africa, traveling to Zambia, Zimbabwe, and Tanzania with equal lack of success, then began looking for black South African actors living in America and Europe. In each case where the candidate met the physical qualifications, his acting was below par, and where the acting was satisfactory the physical characteristics were wrong.

Then began the search for black actors who were not African, and many were considered in Britain, Europe, and America. Some were screen-tested or auditioned, but only one looked to have what was sought—Denzel Washington.

Attenborough had been impressed by Washington's performance in *A Soldier's Story*. He had sensed the kind of screen power he wanted in the Biko role and had arranged to meet Washington, and during this meeting in New York he had been impressed with Washington's "listening" attitude. "It has been said that listening is one of the hardest things to act on the screen," said Attenborough. "This man's quiet strength of presence, the way he leaned against a mantelpiece . . . the way he listened—made me confident that he was a possible Biko for the film if we couldn't find exactly the right African actor."

When this had finally proved to be the case, Denzel Washington was invited to London for further discussions.

On the day I first met Denzel Washington he had not seemed to me an obvious choice for the part of Biko. He was tall, but not quite as tall as Biko had been. He was also slimmer than Biko, and walked and moved differently. Biko had had a kind of bulky presence, and a distinctive manner of movement and gesture. Then there was the question of accent. We had to have an African accent, and Denzel Washington couldn't have sounded more American.

Then some surprising things started to happen. Attenborough asked him to put on a lot of weight during the next two months; his shoes were built up, adding to his height; he started listening to tapes of Biko speaking and practiced the Biko manner and cadence, and he also watched a video of Biko during an interview.

We had an unexpected bonus in the matter of appearance. I had remarked what a pity it was that his teeth were so perfectly spaced, because Biko had had a distinctive gap between his two upper front teeth.

"So have I!" smiled Denzel, explaining that what we saw was a dental fitting used for his work on the television series *St. Elsewhere*, which he would have removed. He did—and there was the gap.

When all this physical transformation was complete, including a Biko-style beard, the effect was remarkable, and when the wardrobe department had dressed him in Biko-style clothes and he had on the broad watch-strap Steve Biko invariably wore, he really did evoke Steve Biko in appearance.

But what was even more remarkable to me than this physical transformation was the way in which Denzel Washington assumed the Biko personality in his general manner, and how this was heightened when he stepped in front of the cameras. The skill in his acting was that he did not appear to be acting, but to be behaving as he had behaved all his life. He acquired that quality of stillness, of quiet power, which Biko had had, and someone else who had known Biko well was amazed at Washington's portrayal. "It's uncanny," he said. "It's as if he *is* him."

I felt the same way during the shooting, and by the time we were halfway through Denzel Washington's scenes I was convinced no other actor could have bettered his performance as Biko. I was interested that Attenborough had been able to see from Washington's performance in *A Soldier's Story*, in which he had played a totally different role, what took me until the full Denzel Washington transformation to see—that quality of quiet power we so crucially needed in the actor to play Biko.

For the role of Wendy, Attenborough had wanted Penelope Wilton from the beginning. Attenborough's son Michael had suggested her (as he had suggested Ben Kingsley for the role of Gandhi), but at the time Penelope had been committed to a contract at the National Theatre. We screen-tested more than a dozen actresses—all of whom I thought were good. Then Penelope's arrangement with the National fell through and she became available. When she was screen-tested none of us had the slightest doubt that she was perfect for the role.

The matter was wrapped up while Attenborough had an appointment with his dentist. He arranged to meet Penelope at the dentist's, no doubt so that the dental plate-twirl wouldn't hold back the plate-twirl involving the approval of lead actress.

For the Woods role Kevin Kline had been on the provisional casting list from the beginning. We had all seen him in *Sophie's Choice*, in which he had brilliantly played the role of the manic Nathan, and he had also been highly praised for his performances in *The Big Chill* and *Silverado* and as the Pirate King in *Pirates of Penzance*. But it was after Attenborough went to New York to see his *Hamlet* that he would have no one else. He came back and reported that Kline was one of the best actors he had seen. A friend of Attenborough's went further and described him as "one of the three best actors in the English-speaking world"; the New York theater press had hailed him as "the American Olivier."

Kevin Kline was brought to London for discussions, and when they had finished giving him gray hair, rimless spectacles, and the kind of clothes I had worn in South Africa in 1977, his acting and dialect skills did the rest. He proved a conscientious researcher, plying us constantly with questions and trying out pronunciation variations at all times and hours.

3
BACK TO AFRICA

A s the Air Zimbabwe plane in which Susie Figgis and I were flying to join the others crossed over the Congo River and then the southern region of Zaire and Zambia, I began to feel conscious that I was close to my first return to Southern Africa since my escape nearly nine years before.

I was unprepared for the effect this return had on me.

I think I had been too busy in exile to have time for homesickness. Landing in exile with a wife and five children and less than a thousand dollars in all the world wonderfully concentrated the mind, and from January 1978 to May 1986 my life had seemed a constant helter-skelter of article-writing, book-writing, lecture tours, political activism, and free-lance journalism, including every little radio broadcast or television interview I could pick up on commission.

From a world in which I had been able to rely on secretaries to type my articles, handle correspondence, pay bills, organize car insurance, and generally make life easy, while on the desk at the end of every month plopped a fat paycheck for me to take home to a spacious house in which servants did the cooking and hard work, it was a far cry to cramped quarters in a London mews where washing up, cleaning, bed making, garbage removal, and cooking was all do-it-yourself, and everything seemed so expensive—especially when there was little money to pay for it.

It had been good for us as a family to enter the real world with its real work and real economy, but financially it had meant the equivalent of treading water just to keep pace with expenditure, and such luxuries as the time for two rounds of golf a week, the occasional poker game, and some serious competitive chess were now just laughable memories of a dream world long forgotten.

And one couldn't ever refuse to help other exiles who weren't being commissioned to write articles or appear on television; one couldn't withhold support for antiapartheid rallies or meetings or campaigns, and one couldn't think of declining to use what would probably be media attention of short duration to counter South African government propaganda, so there was little time for regrets.

We had, during our first week in exile in London, received a blunt warning from the head of South Africa's Security Police, conveyed by special courier. It was to the effect that we should not now think we were "beyond the reach" of his men, and that we were on no account to take part in antiapartheid campaigns. Wendy and I had discussed this and concluded it was probably an attempt to intimidate us rather than a serious threat; that if we yielded to it we would be abdicating for a long time our independence of action, and that the best course would be to defy it as openly as possible. So we made a point of accepting every invitation to speak in public, on radio or television or in person, against apartheid, and both of us traveled wherever such invitations took us. Mine took me as far as the United States and Australia in those first two months, and Wendy's to Europe. In the end the Security Police threat proved to have been a bluff, as had the threat to force our plane down when we flew from Lesotho to Botswana at the time of our escape.

In view of all this activity from the time of going into exile, the years had rolled by with astonishing speed, and I never seemed to have had the leisure to suffer what many exiles experience—the deep longing for home. Yet here, as the aircraft approached Harare, I was starting to realize how unprepared I had been for the emotional impact of returning, not to South Africa, but to right next door—to Southern Africa, with its similarity of scenery and vegetation. After we landed and I stepped off the plane the feel of the place hit me, the clear sky, the benevolent warmth of the winter sun, the fresh smell of the earth, the brightness of the bougainvillea and the familiar look and manner of the people.

The effect was physical. I felt ill and had to go to bed for several hours. But I recovered that afternoon and was able to relish the experience and enjoy my first look at independent Zimbabwe.

Recce to Zimbabwe

I had known this country well in the days when it was called Rhodesia, and as a schoolboy had gone on vacations with friends from Bulawayo. The train from Kimberley used to take two days, and in the early hours of morning would stop at tiny sidings in Botswana called Magalapi and Palapi. There, on a circle of cement in the middle of nowhere at two A.M., would be a jazz quintet of blacks in tuxedos, playing for coins from the passengers.

Rhodesia had always seemed a more broad-minded place than South Africa. The liquor laws were more lax, and schoolboys relished the cheap cigarettes you could get here—Tip-Top were ten for a penny, Zig-Zag were twelve, and Tom-Tom fourteen—and the bartenders weren't so reluctant to sell beer to teenagers. The adults (white) were among the world's most dedicated drinkers, and the cocktails used to come out as early as 4:30 in the afternoon, euphemistically called "sundowners." It seemed to me then a place of perpetual tennis parties, pretty girls, and palatial homes. There had been many servants, but as a young white South African I had hardly noticed them.

The Rhodesians at our school had been different. There had been about sixty of them, and because of their origins they had been excused from Afrikaans lessons. They all seemed to have English names and to be more "English" in their ways than the rest of us. Their money looked different, the coins having a hole in the middle like doughnuts, and their remote roads had tarred strips just wide enough for the wheels of cars, which while better than our worst dirt tracks in South Africa could be tricky for passing or overtaking other cars.

Physically it was a beautiful country, full of tourist attractions, and my hosts used to take me to some of these—the Victoria Falls, more impressive than Niagara because of the volume of water concentrated in the Zambezi Gorge; the Zimbabwe ruins, the remains of an old African citadel in mortarless stone; the Matopo Hills, which were like the roof of the world; the eastern highlands of Inyanga, like Austria in central Africa; and the strange balancing rocks in many regions. There was also Lake Kariba, resulting from the Kariba Dam whose road systems were surveyed by following the elephant tracks.

I remembered from those early visits that although I was more than a thousand miles from home I could understand what the blacks around Bulawayo were saying, because they were Ndebele, descendants of the Nguni who comprised the majority of blacks in Southern Africa and were cultural first cousins to our Zulus, Xhosas, and Swazis. The Ndebele were a minority inhabiting the southwestern region of Zimbabwe centered on Bulawayo. Most of them supported the leadership of Joshua Nkomo, who at the time of filming was engaged in talks with Prime Minister Robert Mugabe to unite the two black factions. Mugabe led the majority Shona group, centered on Harare. The Shona were by repute more politically astute and more "laid back" than the more extroverted Ndebele, and we were to find this reflected in our filming operations. In Harare the crowds were orderly but reserved, whereas in Bulawayo the crowds were exuberant and simulated the fighting scenes with, at times, alarming enthusiasm. This was good for filming but occasionally bad for the nerves.

Susie Figgis and I were met at the airport in Harare by Norman Spencer, who had arrived a few days earlier with the Attenboroughs. We were taken to the Harare Sheraton, a new hotel with a kind of space-age design. It looked like a bronze section of the NASA installation near Houston. Jack Briley was there, along with Kevin Kline, Terry Clegg, and other members of the film unit.

We were taken around the proposed Harare locations, then flew to other locations in various parts of Zimbabwe in a Britten-Norman Islander like the one my family and I had flown in from Lesotho to Botswana. It was strange to be in Harare after knowing it as Salisbury, when it had seemed like the last refuge of the English raj. The Salisbury Club had had a glass slot in the door of the snooker room with a sign: WAIT FOR THE STROKE, and members had sworn that if black rule threatened they would fight to the death against it—yet here many of them still were, still drinking gin and tonic and waiting for the stroke.

Bumping around in the sky in the small plane, with the Attenboroughs dozing arm-in-arm as if still back in Richmond Green, I thought of the lengths to which film people went to make movies, and of how we cinemagoers settled into our plush seats neither knowing nor caring about the depths of determination which took people like these to India and Zimbabwe and other ends of the earth to prepare what we would watch in air-conditioned comfort. Involved though I was in this film, I knew that as a way of life it was not for me.

I had been unprepared for the shock of discovering how hard film people worked. The long hours, from early dawn to late at night; the grinding repetition, the relentless thoroughness, the detailed concentration. I had imagined that being technical consultant on this film would be a leisurely business for me, leaving me free for several hours of writing a day; that I would occasionally be summoned to the set to answer a query like: "How many buttons on a South African police uniform?"

What a laugh . . .

These workaholics required everyone to rise at cock crow, spend every moment physically present on the set within listening distance of the action, concentrate on everything, know everything, and stay through blistering heat or nightly chill until the last cry of: "It's a wrap!" Then, after viewing rushes and tumbling into bed, to wake what felt like ten minutes later to do the same thing. Every day for four months.

Even during that reconnaissance visit to Zimbabwe or "recce" (as the crew called it), I began to get the message, and relayed it to Wendy on my return to London. "Listen," I said. "We are going to have to go along with every inch of this film. We may seldom be called on to do anything beyond getting up out of a canvas chair to answer a question, but we are going to have to be with every development, every scene, every take, every line of dialogue, and every nuance. Not both of us all the time, but one of us all the time. And both of us a lot of the time."

And so it was. Not since boarding school had I had to get up so early for so many consecutive days for so long. But we wouldn't have missed any of it, not only because it was stimulating and enjoyable to watch these experts creating reality out of illusion, but because we were conscious from the beginning that once a scene was shot it was trapped in celluloid, and barring huge expense could not be redone—and if any cock-up resulted from the missing of any crucial detail it would be *our* fault. That, too, wonderfully concentrated the mind.

Final Obstacles

When we had finished looking at the Zimbabwe locations, Attenborough dictating notes about various sets and various scenes, we had an unexpected shock. We believed we had touched all the necessary political bases to clear the project, with broad approval from groups representing most black South Africans; in his visit to South Africa Attenborough had secured the most important endorsement of all, that of Steve Biko's widow and mother. Rightly or wrongly, we felt that the less we communicated details of progress in the project thereafter to the key people inside South Africa whose goodwill we most valued, the more it would protect them from government suspicion of involvement in the film, and that until we had the entire project ready for shooting, with a completed script and all the last financial details in place, it would be better to maintain a minimum of contact.

But we had underestimated the capacity of the South African government and its agencies to capitalize on the long period of noncommunication between us and some of Steve Biko's associates since the Attenborough visit. Somebody conveyed the impression to the Biko family that our film was going to include material damaging to the honor of the family, specifically that we were going to write an extramarital Biko love affair into the script in order to make the film more "commercial," and that Biko's political stance was going to be distorted for commercial ends, making it more "pacifist" in order to please Western audiences.

42

Fortunately we were able to get in touch with Ntsiki Biko and others and, through a complicated arrangement, to show close confidants of theirs the completed script, proving these accusations false and showing that our film was not a political biography of Biko, but was on a broader antiapartheid theme in which elements of the Biko story were included. In retrospect we realized we should have found a way during the previous months of communicating information to those inside without endangering them. This would have made it impossible or at least difficult for malicious persons to have sown doubts in their minds. People living inside South Africa, even the most politically aware people, didn't know how comprehensively they were brainwashed and misinformed of developments outside through cowed media or by increasingly sophisticated means of personal disinformation.

Some of the reports in the South African newspapers were amazing. An early example was the suggestion that Steve Biko was to be played by Paul Newman with his face blackened! Then there were various reports that I had been paid "millions of dollars" to allow my books to be distorted for a "commercial" film—an irony in view of the long battle to stop various producers distorting the story for commercial reasons.

Then a South African producer attacked Attenborough for not filming in South Africa. He said there was still "freedom" in that country to film such a project, and announced that he himself was going to make a film called *Biko—The True Story*. Apparently he went ahead and tried, until his offices were raided by the Security Police and he had to abandon his strange notion.

An American producer was reported as saying he planned to make such a film in South Africa, and he called on a member of the South African cabinet to gain governmental cooperation (obviously neither of these producers had in mind the kind of picture we meant to make), only to be met with a government veto. It soon emerged that both these men had been collaborating on the same project when it collapsed.

Then one of South Africa's biggest newspapers carried a detailed report of what purported to be an attack on our project by one of Steve Biko's close friends. When I telephoned him he said the newspaper concerned had never even contacted him, let alone sought his views.

Then South African radio programs beamed into Zimbabwe began

43

a series of vicious attacks on Attenborough and me, calling on black Zimbabweans to reject white troublemakers like us. Fortunately the black Zimbabweans hadn't been force-fed on crude propaganda like this for years. They laughed off these broadcasts.

Finally there was one highly sophisticated attempt to get the Zimbabwe government to withdraw cooperation and backing from our film. The Zimbabwe officials saw through this as well, though it had been disguised as a radical black approach from radical black South Africans to the radical black Zimbabwe government. (As Senator Edward Kennedy found on his 1984 visit to South Africa, the South African government does not always use white demonstrators or critics to discredit the opponents it fears. Cooperative blacks are more effective.)

The near-hysterical attacks on us and on the film, even before shooting could start, showed how much the South African government feared our project. They had reason, and as we completed our "recce" visit to make preparations for the start of shooting several weeks later, I thought we could expect more than media attacks when we got going on location. In fact, I thought it highly improbable that we would get through our shooting schedule in Zimbabwe without encountering some sort of direct attack against the project by the South African government—either against our sets or equipment, or against ourselves. We were, after all, to spend several months in Zimbabwe, right next door to South Africa, and within easy striking distance.

Though most of the British members of the unit were aware of this possibility, they gave no indication of concern. Sir Richard certainly was aware of it, but showed no sign of worry. He might have been Rhett Butler himself, in that his attitude was: "Frankly, my dear, I don't give a damn." Whether this was fact or illusion only he knew. He was a purveyor of both.

Attenborough had said: "In cinema you sometimes have to perpetrate a lie in order to tell the truth," meaning that scenes sometimes had to be cut out of chronology to avoid audience confusion, or that illusion had to be employed through the camera in order to convey what was fact.

It was, in fact, the exciting art of visual illusion as practiced by some of the world's best filmmakers that I most looked forward to watching as we prepared to start filming in Zimbabwe.

The unit had grown to startling proportions by the time we began shooting in Harare on July 14, 1986. I kept seeing new faces and learning of new functions on the production.

The complex of production offices was like a military headquarters—several acres in downtown Harare containing offices, storerooms, action vehicles, costumes, and maintenance equipment—and a tall radio mast had been erected so that contact could be maintained with far-flung locations during the three months we would be in Zimbabwe.

Strolling through this complex I came around a corner to see an ominous sight—two black Chrysler Valiant cars with CE license plates (East London, South Africa). The color and make of car meant South African Security Police, 1977. It was like stepping backward in time, and though I was to see those black Valiants often during the next three months it was always an uncomfortable experience. It was said that the Security Police now used different makes of cars, but in 1977 the black Valiants had been their sinister trademark.

What was pleasant about seeing them in this context was the relative safety of the new environment. It was like seeing a dangerous snake behind the glass of a snake park rather than in an open field. Though I was aware we were fairly near the South African border, there was such a confident atmosphere of invulnerability about the unit that it rubbed off on me. Attenborough, Clegg, and Tomblin walked about as if the South African government wouldn't dare do anything to them, and this confidence was infectious . . . to some extent.

Then I saw my own car parked in the grounds with the other action vehicles—in fact, two identical copies of what had been my car in South Africa in 1977—again with the appropriate license plate. One was an ordinary 1977 Mercedes, and the other, without wheels or engine, was mounted on a kind of trailer platform behind a camera car with a small rain-making machine poised above it.

This was a strange week in my life. My car, my house, my children, my dog, my wife, and myself—all duplicated!

In the case of the house, there were two duplications. There was a set back at Shepperton Studios for interior shots, and one in Harare mainly for exteriors. The one in Harare was in Ridge Road in the prosperous suburb of Avondale, where the unit had found a vacant site and built the whole thing from plans drawn by the production designer,

Stuart Craig, who had gone to South Africa and seen my former house. It wasn't an exact copy—filmmakers being more interested in camera angles and cinematic effect—but it did have much of the look of the real house, with a two-story bay window running up the corner, a paved courtyard, white walls, double garage, and "maid's" quarters.

Our real house had been bigger but this one was more "upmarket," especially inside. The real house in East London had been the result of an excessive phase I had gone through when I had wanted a Mediterranean-type villa and had given the architect a rough sketch for him to turn into design art. He had succeeded, and we had ended up with a big white house with thick walls, terrace, swimming pool, arches, and an atrium courtyard with a fountain. On hot days the water used to splash coolly—when I remembered to switch it on.

The Harare one was so attractive that several prospective buyers made inquiries about the price—until they walked around the back and saw nothing but scaffolding and plywood backing. It was mostly a façade, but the outside on three sides looked fine, and inside were only two completed rooms with the other interior doors leading nowhere.

The one at Shepperton, being mostly for interior shots, looked great on the inside but was scaffold and rough boarding on the outside. It was like the Harare house turned inside out. But they had identical courtyards and trellis bougainvillea (made of silk) and, astonishingly, identical views. The views in Harare were genuine, and in Shepperton fake, though the difference was undetectable on film because of a new process in which the backdrops were giant color transparencies through which powerful lights shone to give the quality of Southern African light.

I had asked Attenborough why he didn't save money by filming some exterior scenes in England, saying that while taking our daughter Jane to Norwich for the university term we had seen a long stretch of motorway that was identical to part of the road between East London and King William's Town in South Africa. The countryside had seemed strikingly similar. When the British Settlers had arrived in South Africa in 1820 the eastern province where they had landed by sailing ship had countryside so like England, with green rolling hills, that they had called the place Albany. Attenborough had shaken his head regretfully: "It's the quality of the light," he said. "There is a totally different quality of light in South Africa." I hadn't thought the difference would be noticeable, but he was emphatic that it would. A storage room at the production office had been converted into a makeshift viewing theater, with eggboxes lining the walls for soundproofing, so that we could see the printed takes of film after quick processing. These are called "rushes" in Britain and "dailies" in America, and with my mid-Atlantic proclivities I took to calling them "daily rushes." Their purpose was a quick check so that the director could approve the scenes as photographically acceptable as to focus and clarity before the set could be broken up.

4

ON LOCATION

On the first morning of filming we all set out in convoy from the Harare Sheraton hotel, most of the unit in warm clothing because the sun wasn't properly up yet. When we arrived at Ridge Road to do the first scene I was excited to see the trucks with the cables and generator parked beside the set, the tent town for the crew facilities over the hill, and the caravans for the actors, hairdressers, wardrobe, and administration staff. People were charging about with a sense of purpose and all sorts of mysterious things appeared to be happening without actually happening, or were actually happening without appearing to be happening.

Most of the activity seemed to be centered on the lighting arrangements, which took more than two hours, while Attenborough and his camera operator walked about looking at things from different angles. From time to time one of them would make an odd gesture with his index and middle fingers extended in a V shape parallel to the ground, and they would all nod vigorously. Then another would make the same sort of illustrative movement, this time with the index and little finger extended, or with the roots of two index fingers joined with the tips splayed outward. This, it transpired, was a simulation of the camera viewpoint dimension, the wide ends of the V representing the parameters of vision in the frame.

"What's going on?" I asked Patrick Kinney.

"Oh, the lighting takes a long time, balancing indoor and exterior lighting, and there are subsequent camera angles to work out while that goes on. There's a lot of preparation and it takes a long time. There's an old saying about filming—Hurry up and wait!"

Finally came the magic call of: "Right—turn over!" and Attenborough's first strangled shout of: "Aaaaaction!"

His various styles of calling "Action!" were soon to be familiar. One was quietly insistent, as if reminding someone of something: "Action?" Another was decisive, as if the last word in an argument in which no further discussion would be tolerated: "*AK*-shun!" (This one was in two notes, the second syllable being almost an octave lower.) Then there was a very soft one, barely audible, when he felt the mood of the actor was perfect and not to be disrupted by raised voices. It was almost as tender as the whisper of a lover: "Action, darling . . . ?"

But usually it was explosive, a harsh shout of exultant command: "*Ughghghghghgh-kshunnnnnn!*" This one sent birds flying from trees and startled sleeping dogs, resounding through the set to galvanize the actors into performance.

The first scene we shot that morning was of Kevin Kline looking out of a window at the two Security Police watching the house—"my" house . . .

After helping to raise a fuss about the killing of Steve Biko I had been banned—forbidden to speak publicly or move about freely—and the Security Police had kept watch on the house to maintain the pressure of surveillance. The first scene was designed by Briley to convey the sense of being a prisoner in my own house, and I was interested in how Attenborough would shoot to achieve the desired effect.

The way he chose was illuminating, and I realized on that first morning that he had the ability to maximize the scenes in the script cinematically, to go beyond the written word to convey the image.

Kevin Kline had been asked not to shave that morning, so that when he looked out of the window it reinforced the impression of a man confined to his house; a man with no "office" to go to and no formal appointments to keep. It was done initially as an optical illusion. First you saw the image of the Security Police and the black Valiant, then you realized they were being reflected in a window, and when Kline's face appeared at the window he was looking through Venetian blinds which gave a barred effect.

I realized then that, good as I had thought the script to be, the actual film would be even more powerful because of the extra quality the director could give it through imaginative use of the camera and the skill of the actors.

I had the same feeling about the next scene—a reconstruction of the incident in which I was served with a subpoena requiring me to name a witness to a Security Police crime or go to prison. I had told the minister of police, J. T. Kruger, that his Security Police had been seen vandalizing Biko's Black Community Centre, and after telling me he would pursue the matter Kruger had instead approved a subpoena against me. Watching Kevin Kline reenacting this gave me a first insight into acting. There was Kevin, a Midwestern American who had never been subjected to this sort of thing, conveying by his facial expression, manner of speaking, and even the look in his eyes precisely the feelings I had had that day—and his South African accent was good.

This was the first airing of Kline's South African accent. He had gone to a phonetics coach in New York, had listened to tapes, and had taped Wendy and me as well to copy our intonations. He was therefore able to meet Attenborough's requirement that he speak like a South African. Good musicians are usually good mimics, and Kevin Kline had studied at Juilliard and was a talented pianist. His keen ear had picked up many of the characteristics of our South African way of speech, so when the Security Police officer stated that his orders to issue the subpoena came "from the top," Kline said, "Kruger?" pronouncing it as I had, "Krewga?"

Whites in South Africa have two basic accents—the heavily accented English spoken by Afrikaners, and the English spoken by English-speaking descendants of the British. The latter is ours, and it sounds to some foreigners like a blend of Australian and Cockney. Americans think it sounds British, and the British think it sounds foreign. The thing the British notice most about the way we speak is our pronunciation of *oo* sounds, which are thin and flat. Instead of "I like you too" we would say something like "Ah lahk yew tew." Norman Spencer was perpetually amused at the way I pronounced *here* as "hyuh" (a short, abrupt syllable), whereas the British protract the word to "hee-ah."

The subpoena scene followed closely what had been said and done on the day I had been called to my front door and given the shock of the threat of imprisonment. The real-life Security Police officer that day had been a Colonel Van de Merwe, whose dark glasses had given him a sinister appearance. The actor playing him, Miles Anderson, was also in dark glasses, and having been born in our part of the world he had the Afrikaans accent just right. In fact the scene looked and sounded so authentic that I felt nervous all over again watching it.

I had to watch it a lot. I hadn't realized how often a scene had to be repeated for different camera setups, not because of mistakes but because of how films were made, and I now began to see how the process worked.

A film is like a completed jigsaw puzzle designed by the director, and to give him a range of options on how the final result will look each of the puzzle pieces has to be made in alternative ways. And if the complete film can be likened to a completed jigsaw puzzle, the shooting can be likened to the making of all the individual pieces. Each piece is a scene, and each scene consists of camera setups from different angles and distances. And each setup can require a number of "takes," sometimes up to twenty.

If a scene is, say, of four people arguing—call them Matthew, Mark, Luke, and John—first there will be a general shot, called the master shot, of the whole argument. Then come the detailed shots, the individual close-ups. First a close-up of Matthew, from right in front of his face, the whole scene gone through again with all the actors speaking their lines as before. Two or three or more printed takes of this will be ordered by the director, then each of the others—Mark, Luke, and John—will get their close-up turn. Each of these requires its own lighting arrangement, and of course a different camera setup, so the argument scene might take an entire day to film from every angle and aspect, although the final edited scene might last no more than a minute and a half.

When we cinemagoers see that ninety seconds of film on the screen, we are seeing the final scene provided after the director and film editor have joined up the pieces they want, cut and shaped as they choose. We might see five seconds of the general scene of the argument, then, as Matthew makes a telling point, a close-up of his face for perhaps four seconds, then the reaction of the others, and as Mark, Luke, and John interjected we would cut in turn to the close-ups of each of them. The effect is of a fast-paced argument in which, because we are brought close to it by the camera from time to time, we feel we were almost participants, while the general view gives us the wider perspective of the onlooker. The skill of the director and the film editor will determine the right mix of involvement or detachment for the audience.

Whatever the scene in a film, the procedure is basically the same—a blend of general shots with particular close-ups or at least shots from different angles—so that in order to shape the jigsaw-puzzle piece the editor has to have all the various ingredients available in the form of separate printed takes from the different points of view determined by the director. This is why it would take four months to shoot a film which would end up lasting about two and a half hours—the final edited version, called the "final cut," being the compacted joining together of all the edited scenes.

After watching the first day's shooting in Harare I realized why filmmakers regard it as productive to end up with a minute and a half of edited film per day. It takes as much as half an hour or more of unedited film to produce that minute and a half of edited film, and to shoot half an hour of unedited film takes something like five hours of prelighting and camera setup involving the laying of camera tracks or the construction and positioning of a camera platform.

Attenborough was infinitely patient and thorough about rehearsing the actors, sensitive to the fact that different actors required different styles and types of rehearsal. Often he was to be seen quietly talking and attentively listening as one of the actors wanted a long discussion about a scene. This, like the lighting, was time-consuming. Yet he kept

Oscar-winning scriptwriter John Briley with co-producer
Norman Spencer, on location. *(Simon Mein)*

Denzel Washington asks Donald Woods about Biko's approach to rugby and is told: "He was a dirty player!" *(Simon Mein)*

Denzel Washington, who plays Biko, checks script with Attenborough. *(Simon Mein)*

Attenborough
consults Wendy
and Donald Woods
about the shooting
of a scene.

Sound recordist Simon Kaye *(left)* lends the earphones to Woods and Attenborough to check accents with Wendy Woods and Kevin Kline on the right.

Attenborough with director of cinematography
Ronnie Taylor, cameraman Eddie Collins, stand-by
Jim Kerr, and production designer Stuart Craig,
composing a shot. *(Simon Mein)*

Denzel Washington as Steve Biko and Kevin Kline as Donald Woods in an early scene from the movie.

Kline and Washington in Biko's
Daily Dispatch office.

to the day's schedule and at the end of the location shooting period we had met the target set at the start of production.

Lighting, rehearsal, and movement and positioning of equipment and vehicles were all part of the preparation for shooting a scene, and it was obviously a complex operation requiring specialist skills of the highest order.

What we were watching that morning was the creation in rough of the first jigsaw-puzzle pieces to be set aside and cut to fit into their place in the completed film. At this stage the editing was no concern of Attenborough's. For the next four months he would be concerned only with shooting all the scenes. Only later in London, when finished with the actors and camera crew and all the other business of shooting, would he settle down with the film editor, Lesley Walker, to "join it all together." That operation, in addition to the dubbing, soundtrack, and music, would take a further five months.

Lighting was obviously more important in filming than I had realized. Here we all were, a large group of people involved in an operation costing more than $50,000 a day, depending in large measure for the pace of production on one man—the "lighting cameraman." The head of the camera team, Ronnie Taylor, was deceptively titled because he seldom touched or operated the camera. More correctly he was called director of photography, or cinematographer. Apart from the director, he had the pivotal job in the unit, and the job that most combined the technical with the artistic: he had to see to it that the lighting was right for every camera setup and every take for every scene. Ronnie had won an Oscar for his cinematography for *Gandhi* and had also worked with Attenborough on *A Chorus Line*, so they knew each other's way well and worked together smoothly.

Lighting each scene could take hours, because on a quality film only the best photography will do. The huge screens used in the best cinemas show everything in a scene in such detail that the shortcuts commonly taken in productions for television, with its much smaller screen, can't be taken in a feature film. The lighting cameraman is therefore an artist, and each scene is a picture requiring as much composition in light as ever an old master painter had to consider.

The cinematographer has to provide clarity without excess. He has to deceive, because even a night scene can't be completely dark, or the audience would see nothing. They have to be deceived into accepting that they can see in the dark, without their being aware of the deception. Therefore sources of light have to make sense. A night scene might require more light than one streetlight could provide, so the audience has to be persuaded to accept more light from that streetlight without noticing the fact—perhaps through a suggestion of moonlight, or flashes of light from passing cars. Then during the day in bright sunlight the camera can't just shoot an interior scene without the external light being filtered—the door and windows would show up as abnormally blurred wedges of exaggerated light. Ronnie Taylor had to work out all these balances, and to put up screens and filters in order to make the finished scene look normal.

Lights couldn't simply be placed—they had to be screened from reflecting off surfaces in the scene. Often you would see a light with a black shield called a "flag" in front of it, or you would see Ronnie Taylor arranging a reflector screen so that the light could be bounced indirectly onto the scene for a more diffuse effect.

During outdoor scenes Ronnie was often heard calling for "some dingle"—bits of branch and shrub which were erected to cast shadows on white walls to break up the glare of the surface or to create an effect. Sometimes "dingle" was used to disguise a light stand or other item of equipment that might show up in a scene.

Textbooks have been written on the subject of cinema lighting, but it is like the art of the chef. It can't be learned from books, only from experience and intuition.

Because production depended so much on lighting, Ronnie Taylor could never relax completely on the set. He was always either setting up the lighting for a scene or supervising the shooting of the scene; immediately thereafter setting up the lighting for the next scene . . . He seldom looked at people, only into spaces, and seemed to take note of objects only insofar as they reacted to light. He would pad about with the gait of a bear, bent forward from the waist, with a light meter hanging from his neck, and his first action on preparing to light a scene would be to call for Alan Martin, the chief electrician. "Alan!" he would call plaintively on a rising note, then *"Al!"* to order certain lights in certain places, sometimes scratching his head before brandishing the light meter in the appropriate direction.

His even temperament and quiet good humor on that first day of shooting was to be maintained throughout the four months of filming, and it seemed remarkable that the one person who could least relax on the set was one of the most relaxed members of the unit in his general demeanor.

It was soon obvious that the heart of the unit was the camera crew. They were a special breed apart, and I was told this was always the case on a film. There was a journalistic parallel. In all my years on newspapers, including twelve years as an editor, the subeditors were the princes of the establishment. The "subs' table" was "where it was at" as they condensed and headlined the copy of lesser drones and designed news-page layouts while getting their own tea and evolving their own in-jokes. On this project I found the camera crew were the equivalent of the "subs," with their own esprit de corps and sense of style. A mischievously unreliable source of information on such matters as times of rushes or scenes to be shot, or even days to be worked, they were, like a good subs' table, the heartbeat of the operation, and the proof of their expertise was the quality of what showed up on the screen.

The most junior member of the camera team, Richard Tindall, was always on the go, fetching and carrying when he wasn't changing the film magazine—a daunting procedure to watch as he thrust his arms into the dark recesses of a lightproof bag to take out the used film roll and put in a new one without mixing the two up, which if he had done it would have cost thousands of dollars in wasted film and time.

As trainee he also had the job of getting tea and sandwiches for the camera crew and forever seemed to be scrambling about with a laden tray in between his technical chores. When not engaged in this or helping to man the camera, he was scrawling the scene and take numbers on the clapperboard and scrambling to "clapper" or slate on cue before each take. This was a necessary procedure so that the soundtrack could be timed from the sound of the clapper, for synchronization with the picture, and so the takes could be identified by number for the film editor.

Richard had long wanted this job, and had qualified to get it partly because he had buried some puppies which had died. He had heard whining sounds in the night, and after a long search had found several newborn puppies, two of which had died of exposure in the cold. Rescuing the live ones, he had gone out again to bury the dead ones, and a woman observing this had been impressed with his compassion. More than a year later, in another city, he had applied for a job on a film crew, and the woman doing the initial hiring had turned out to be the woman who had seen him burying the puppies. She recognized him and got him his first job in films.

Richard's trainer as official clapper-loader was a quiet young man named Steve Burgess, one of the few members of this golf-conscious unit who couldn't be prevailed on to play golf. The rest of us hacked around the course at various levels of competence or incompetence along with several of the Zimbabweans on the film who were very good. Camera grip David Chiganze was a six handicap, Eli Fero of the accounts department was a three, and one of the stand-ins, Jimmy Tavengwa, was actually a plus one, but Steve Burgess wasn't interested. Then it was discovered that he was a former golf professional who had grown sick of the game, and thereafter he never stood a chance of escaping the course. Initially he only consented to coach some of us, but in the process he recaptured his interest in the game, and by the end of the shooting the golf fever had him again.

Another keen golfer on the camera crew was the key grip, the man in charge of those lifting and carrying the camera into position and of pivotal importance in controlling the physical movement of the camera on mobile shots, on the dolly or crane and along tracks. He had to ensure that the pace and type of camera movement were just right, and he was one of the most sought-after key grips in the world. This was a red-haired Irishman with a look of perpetual mischief, Jimmy Waters. Jimmy came from a family of twenty-one children—all from the same mother and father—and had yet to meet some of his brothers and sisters as he had left home at fourteen.

He had left because home in Tipperary was a small farmhouse with only two bedrooms, one for the parents and one for the children, crammed into two double beds with the overflow accommodated in the barn. "I got tired of falling out of bed and not being able to get back in," he said, and as I began to smile at the joke I saw by his expression that it wasn't one. He had left for London to seek his fortune and, after many years spent in perfecting his craft, he had become the founder of Grip House, now the biggest grip company in the world.

On his last visit home his father had told him proudly that a modern new flush toilet had replaced the old outhouse, and when Jimmy went to inspect it he found it had been built nearly a hundred yards from the house, where the old outhouse had been situated.

"Why did you build it out here?" asked Jimmy. "Why isn't it in the house?"

His father replied: "Nobody's ever shat in that house, and nobody ever will!"

Another of the camera-crew characters was Jason Lehel, the focus puller, who had to keep the focus adjusted to the exact distance measured for perfect focus, at times having to work to within an inch of focus over a distance of several yards—no easy matter when an actor was moving quickly into and out of the distance during a lively scene. Any miscalculation by Jason would have resulted in the dreaded "soft focus," wasting the scene and necessitating an expensive retake. Looking like a younger and less shaven version of actor James Caan, Jason Lehel must have been exact over four grueling months, judging by the several thousand printed takes which emerged crisp and clear on the screen.

In the saddle as camera operator was Eddie Collins, a crew-cut cockney frequently consulted by Attenborough before and after takes about the camera position in relation to the actors' movements and about his "feel" for the shot. He had worked with Attenborough on many films as clapper-loader and as focus puller and they obviously enjoyed working together, exchanging jibes and amiable insults as an overlay of their mutual professional respect.

Norman Spencer observed that our film seemed to have more "tracking" shots than most—shots in which the camera moved on rails or on a board to match the movement of the action, and it was surprising to me how quickly Jimmy Waters and his men could lay down the rails of the track, using wedges and spirit levels to keep them on a constant plane.

In fact, the carpenters, riggers, and lighting hands given the generic term "standby" seemed the opposite of the image many people have of the indolent British worker. They worked with impressive speed to assemble platforms for the cameras or the big lights. There were five in particular I came to think of as "the cockney quintet"—Dave McWhinnie, Les Beaver, Bob Betts, George Gibbons, and Jim Kerr—who invariably worked shirtless in the hot Zimbabwe sun and performed prodigies of quick construction while exchanging rapid-fire wisecracks.

During that first day's filming in Harare, Attenborough decided to include an unscripted appearance by one of the best actors in the unit—Charlie the dog.

Playing the part of our family dog Charlie back in South Africa, this highly intelligent animal performed under the guidance of his trainer, Paul Ball, exactly as Attenborough required, and twice the appreciative Sir Richard called him "Charlie darling." He had to help answer the door when the Security Police officer rang to deliver the subpoena threat, which emphasized the contrast between the domestic atmosphere in the house and the sudden note of menace when the purpose of the visit was disclosed.

Actually there were two Charlies. Owing to Britain's quarantine regulations which made it impossible in the time available to take a dog to Zimbabwe and back again to London for studio shooting, we had to have a British Charlie and a Zimbabwean Charlie. And they had to look identical, so a touch of judicious hair-dyeing was necessary.

As was to be expected, the British Charlie was more reserved than the Zimbabwean Charlie. Or it may have been that the Zimbabwean Charlie was more animated than the British Charlie. But I was told that wouldn't be noticed by cinema audiences because the two Charlies shared sequences closely cut together and it would probably have taken a mother of one of them to spot the difference.

It seemed to typify the more lunatic side of filmmaking that a dog could be filmed running out of a room in Southern Africa to emerge six thousand miles away a different dog entirely—yet through the same doorway . . . or what *looked* like the same doorway, because really the *inside* of the door was the same but the *outside* of the door was in a different continent three months later. Yet given the same tail-wag, the same markings, the same cinematic character, and that the whole sequence would take only a few seconds, it would generally be accepted that the two dogs were one dog.

While all this creativity was going on I was feeling hungry, and the lunch break showed that whatever else happened to this unit it would be well fed. Down on the other side of the hill from the set the big tent held rows of tables and cauldrons of good food. There was even pumpkin, which I hadn't tasted since leaving South Africa nine years before.

The caterer was Rob Leslie, whose father, Adam Leslie, had been South Africa's leading political satirist in the sixties. He had delighted the relatively few liberals in the country with his antiapartheid revues, and I had twice been commissioned to write material for his shows. One commission had resulted in "My Dark Lady," in which a member of the South African cabinet had sought to turn a lowly flower seller from the black township into a tribesmaiden in a Bantustan homeland in accordance with government policy. Because the South African parliament fronted a square called Stal Plein, one number had been "The Reign We Gain Stays Mainly in Stal Plein." Others had included "As I Crawl Through the Kraal Where You Live," and the state witch-doctor's song, "I Could Have Tranced All Night."

During the lunch break Attenborough spoke about the difference between film acting and stage acting. He said that when he and his contemporaries went from stage to film in England they had had to learn new techniques, because the camera saw things which theater audiences weren't close enough to see. If you were an actor on the stage you had to "project"—to "act more," because on the stage you were only life-size and the people in the backseats couldn't pick up slight nuances of gesture or expression. But on the cinema screen, especially in close-ups, your face could be twenty feet across and the audience felt you were near them, so in front of the camera you had to do the opposite of stage acting—you had to *under*act; almost *un*act. Gestures, facial and otherwise, had to be underplayed and emotions underprojected.

The cinema professionals said that the camera could read your mind, that all a good actor had to do was *think* an emotion rather than act it, and the understatement somehow made the effect stronger on the screen.

During our time in Zimbabwe Attenborough was often to be heard reminding some of the actors of this. He would "frame" his face with his hands to signify how close the close-up was and say: "We're *here*, darling, so bring it down . . . bring it down."

The actors spoke of the advantage of having a director who had acted. They said he knew their concerns and requirements better than someone who had only been on the other side of the camera. Attenborough himself said he thought there were basically three types of directors, those who were mainly interested in the pyrotechnics of film effect, those who were mainly interested in cinematic image on the screen, and those, like himself, who felt the actors were the most important means of cinematic communication. "I want to get the audiences involved with the actors and convinced by the actors; to encourage the actors to 'relax' in the sense that they will extend themselves even to the point of risking failure."

Terry Clegg said that the way Attenborough worked with actors was uniquely effective. "He could get an emotional response out of a block of wood—and we've had some of those on various films!"

Clegg had an apt turn of phrase. Once, on studying a portrait of Attenborough, he said: "I know that expression so well—it comes just before he asks the question that turns my guts to water!"

As filming resumed after lunch on that first day, I began to get used to the pattern of operation that was emerging. When Attenborough had decided on a camera angle, Ronnie Taylor would start getting the lighting right while Attenborough rehearsed the actors for the camera position. David Tomblin would depute Roy Button and Patrick Kinney to get their runners on the perimeter to stop traffic or noise.

When all was prepared, an increasingly familiar ritual would begin. Attenborough would stand beside the camera lens after looking through it or conferring with Eddie Collins, the grips would get ready for whatever camera movement was wanted, the sound recordist would put on his earphones and switch on, and the clapper-loader would chalk the take number and scene number on the clapperboard. Then David Tomblin would say: "Quiet everyone . . . Turn over!" The sound recordist would say: "Sound speed!" Eddie Collins would say: "Mark it!" The clapper-loader would call out the take and scene numbers, clack the board, and duck away out of sight of the camera. Then Attenborough would lean forward to call: "Action!"

Simon Kaye, who headed the sound department, had often worked with Attenborough before. I asked him why he used the expression *sound speed*. He explained that in the early days of recording the machines had required time to get up to the right speed to suit the filming operation; the phrase had stuck, although technically the speed of the recording tape is no longer a problem in this way.

Wherever we were filming, in the heat of Zimbabwe or Kenya or in the cold of Shepperton, his recording table was always to be seen as near to the "action" as he could get it without obtruding on the set, and his earphones were as much a part of him as those of an airline pilot. He would stand at that table for hours and never seemed to tire of trying for the perfect recording. I was told by other specialists in sound that many films were substantially rerecorded after the final editing, even down to individual voices, but that the ideal was to have as much of the original sound as possible and that Simon Kaye's films had a considerably higher proportion of original sound than most. During the 1987 Academy Awards Simon won an Oscar for his work on *Platoon*. I wasn't surprised at this, after watching him work for four months on our film. His powers of concentration were as impressive as his conscientiousness in recording repeatedly until satisfied as to quality.

He even used to record nothing. That is, to my ears nothing could be heard if there was no dialogue or if there weren't sound effects, but I was told these were "atmosphere tracks," that even apparent silences were not always total silences. If shots later had to be matched up, the quality of the "non-noise" in each had to be identical. Similarly, if there was only slight sound in one shot there had to be similar slight sound in the matching shot. Kaye also had to do "wild-track" recordings: recording off-camera lines which might be useful in the editing of the film.

With Kaye was his accustomed team, Taffy Haines for sound maintenance and Tommy Staples as boom operator. The latter's job, it transpired, was a lot harder than it looked. He wasn't simply holding a long pole with a microphone on the end to catch the actors' lines—he had to get as near as possible without the boom or the microphone showing in the frame or reflecting from any surface or casting any shadow.

Taffy Haines had the job of keeping the recording machines in order. There was no more Welsh Welshman than he. A portly, stocky man with silver-white hair, he had a distinctive walk with arms held akimbo as if ready to defend himself against surprise attack by the English. He was reputed to know more about the insides of tape recorders than you could shake a leek at. From a technical job in the Royal Air Force in World War II he had received special training in sound equipment maintenance, and his presence in Zimbabwe and Kenya was Simon Kaye's guarantee that those delicate machines, six thousand miles from home, would keep functioning at the peak of efficiency.

Close by the sound-recording table, and even closer to the "action," would always be Nikki Clapp. Formally described as script supervisor but more commonly called "continuity," hers was, I thought, the toughest job in the whole unit.

Her job was literally not to miss a thing. If an actor's tie was knotted to the left in a certain scene, it had to be exactly the same way in a matching scene which might be shot six thousand miles away and three months later. She had to note every take, and details of every take, and to record which takes were printed, and to time each scene to the second. More importantly, she had to be sure that in scenes involving five or more people the various complex movements had the basic uniformity from take to take which would ensure that she had succeeded in her chief task: determining that the finished film would "cut together"—that the director and editor wouldn't be confronted by takes that could not possibly be intercut because of inconsistencies of movement or gesture or detail.

She carried a pad to which were clipped many pens in different colors for the notation of different facts, and the minute there was a lull in shooting she would be typing away at a tiny portable to fill in reports of the filming. When it was dark she would wear bizarre yellow spectacles fitted with twin flashlights beaming on the page for her to type by.

Nikki Clapp had done the continuity on *Out of Africa* and had found Meryl Streep a pleasure to work with, but had been less than crazy about Robert Redford. His attitude had been that continuity wasn't an actor's concern, and that if he chose to peel an orange eight different ways in eight takes, that was her problem, not his.

Attenborough was immensely impressed with Nikki Clapp and told me at the end of the film: "She is unsurpassed. I rank her with the very best I have worked with and I would want her with me on every film from now on."

Other things I learned on that first day concerned stand-ins and eyelines. I had always thought an actor's stand-in was someone who could replace the actor, somewhat like an understudy—an absurd thought if you followed it through, because you couldn't replace actors partway through a film as you could during a theater run on the live stage. Theater performances didn't relate to performances on other days or nights—they didn't have to "match up" as in a film.

Doubles, of course, were different. You could use a double in a film, someone of the same height and coloring and general appearance as the actor, for long shots or stunts where there were no close-ups of the face.

But a stand-in was literally that—someone who stood in for the actor while a scene was being worked out for lighting, camera angles, when the focus puller was measuring the exact distances for focus purposes and the camera operator was working out what would be in the frame. This avoided making an actor stand for hours without calling on his acting ability until it was needed. Ideally the stand-in was the same height, build, and general appearance as the actor. No acting ability was required.

The question of the "eyeline" at first was a mystery. David Tomblin would call: "Clear the eyeline!" and I would look about wondering what he meant. Was it an "I-line"? Or possibly an "aye-line"?

It turned out to be the direction the actor was looking in. Actors found it distracting to see the faces of onlookers when they were pretending to be seeing only the person they were talking to. Having the camera crew, director and assistant director, sound recordist, boom operator, and continuity supervisor already there beside the camera could be distracting enough. Even these tried to keep out of the direct eyeline, but it was all the more important for others who didn't have to be in this eyeline to clear out of the way.

The fact that you couldn't replace an actor halfway through a film without reshooting everything up to that point made the safety of the actors paramount, and the actors and other key people in our unit were protected through careful security arrangements—often more protected than they realized. The extra dimension of threat in our case was because of the known hostility of the South African government to our project, and the fact that Zimbabwe, being right next door to South Africa, was occasionally infiltrated by South African agents—and sometimes attacked, as we had seen from the bombings in Harare.

The Zimbabwe government and our production heads had worked out a system of security cooperation, and we were guarded not only by our own security people but by the Zimbabweans as well. One evening at the Ridge Road set a handsome young black couple were watching the filming, and because no unauthorized persons were permitted on the set David Tomblin immediately asked our security people who they were. "Zimbabwe security," came the reply.

On occasion the casual black laborers on the various sets included, though many members of our unit didn't know it, experienced ex-guerrillas with automatic rifles ready to hand.

Naturally the most obvious target for the South Africans was Attenborough himself, so he had to be the most protected. Wherever he went there were always two men in unobtrusive attendance, dressed to blend into the background. Both were former officers of Britain's SAS regiment, highly trained in everything from unarmed combat to split-second crisis situations, as their colleagues had shown in the rescue raid on the Iranian embassy in London several years before.

These two had trained such units not only of the British but also of the American special forces, but apart from looking particularly healthy and fit they didn't stand out obviously among members of the unit as far as strangers were concerned. They were at all times armed with Browning automatics, precisely how I still don't know, because you never saw a bulge in their clothing even when they wore only shorts and a T-shirt. However, I never actually looked into their lunch tins or folded newspapers, and I couldn't swear to it that they were carrying only scripts with them.

"Most of the time we are geared to preventing incidents rather than stopping them," one told me. "My partner's priority is to have an escape drill by which Sir Richard can be got to a car and driven away immediately, while I have to guarantee them time to get away."

Actually they usually didn't call him Sir Richard. Because Attenborough was referred to in memoranda as SRA they called him the phonetic version of that—Sirrah. Thus: "My job is to stop anyone who tries to get at Sirrah, preferably by delaying an attacker rather than killing him. Violence is only a last resort, and a weapon is used only if you can't delay or incapacitate the attacker."

I asked how he would "delay" an attacker.

"Well, there again, it depends what the threat is. If he's just a right-wing drunk or someone with a passing grudge, I'll distract him while my partner gets Sirrah away. And if he gets physical, I'll get in his way physically."

He thought for a while.

"If the threat is really dangerous you have to assess it very quickly and react—again without weapons if possible. But if necessary you have to be prepared to kill him."

"Without weapons?"

"Depends on what he has on him. Obviously if he's pointing a gun at Sirrah and I'm not near enough to disarm him I have to shoot him."

Could a weapon be produced and used against the gunman before the gunman could squeeze the trigger?

Er . . . yes, actually.

"In such a situation you use a heavy-caliber pistol. It has the stopping power, you see. And you always fire at least two rounds—that really throws him back."

Was that the equivalent of being hit by, say, a car?

"No—by a London bus!"

He had himself been hit by such a bullet once, a glancing blow on the wrist, and the force had swung his arm up so violently that his shoulder had been dislocated.

Were there any particular points of special danger for Sir Richard in the location shooting?

65

"Yes, the big crowd scenes at Chibuku Stadium . . . any occasions when there are a lot of people."

Did he and his partner practice their skills?

"Yes, once a week at the firing range, with a variety of weapons, then regular speed-driving and evasion-driving practice, followed by practice in unarmed combat. We keep it up, the two of us."

Who guarded Sir Richard while they were away practicing?

"He is guarded all the time. We have other arrangements—the Zimbabweans have been very helpful."

I later learned that the word had been leaked to Pretoria that in addition to Mr. Mugabe's best security men Sir Richard and the unit had in attendance two members of "the Regiment." I discussed this with the two. They smiled.

"Prevention's better than cure, isn't it?" said one.

5
ANIMALS, WHITE ZIMBABWEANS, AND OTHER DETAILS

Across the street from the Ridge Road set were some fine houses, several of them owned by wealthy whites who had stayed on after Zimbabwe independence. Wendy and I chatted to a number of them, and most were full of praise for the reconciliatory policies of the Mugabe government toward whites. But some felt much had changed for the worse. One said: "Well, they've brought in this minimum-wage business, now. You can't pay a black worker less than a certain figure. I used to employ four servants—now I can only afford two."

This reminded me of whites back in South Africa who said they could only afford to pay low wages; that they would have to dismiss their servants if compelled to pay more—and where would all these unemployed servants find work? At a symposium on the subject one man told a panel which included Archbishop Denis Hurley of Durban: "I can only afford to pay forty rands a month—does that mean I must fire my washerwoman?"

Archbishop Hurley replied: "No—it means you can only afford a washerwoman for two days of the week."

The general impression of most of the unit the longer we stayed in Zimbabwe was that race relations appeared at least on the surface to be remarkably good, considering there had been a fairly recent war in which forty thousand had died. Most of the whites who had stayed on were glad they had, and some who had left for South Africa were trying to get back to Zimbabwe, having jumped from what they thought was the frying pan into what they now realized was the fire.

But there was still a rump of die-hard Ian Smith supporters, generally to be found among the older people who had had a lifetime of racist indoctrination. One such had been my aunt Marjorie. During the Smith regime all "loyal" whites had been asked to send to relatives abroad an air letter on which there was a preprinted section and a vacant section—the latter for personal messages. The printed section urged the recipient not to believe what the newspapers abroad reported about "Rhodesia." It stated that there was no war on; that all was calm, supplies were plentiful, and race relations better than ever. Adding her personal message after this, my loyal but naïve aunt had written: "We're all well, and my grandsons are all fine, though we're worried about them being called up into the army so young, as the casualty rate seems to be increasing."

Two young white Zimbabweans attached to the unit as production runners, Clive Stafford and Peter Bennett, enjoyed baiting Patrick Kinney. Their job was to man the perimeters of the shooting area; to keep traffic redirected and to keep noise levels down. Patrick Kinney would call into his walkie-talkie: "Are you in position, Clive?" and Clive would reply: "Yes, but Peter Bennett isn't," and if Patrick checked with Peter he'd say: "Yes, but Clive isn't."

These two were occasionally a trial to Patrick, who wasn't always aware that he was being hailed by radio as: "Hat-rack," or "Fatrick," or sometimes even "Gatwick."

An enjoyable irony of our film was that many of the whites recruited in Zimbabwe to play the parts of South African soldiers and police were white exiles from South Africa who had opposed apartheid, several of them former political prisoners.

As technical consultants Wendy and I were required to check all

ANIMALS,
WHITE
ZIMBABWEANS,
AND
OTHER
DETAILS

sets and set dressing, and found only one thing wrong at the Ridge Road house. The legs of the bed of Evalina, our "maid" in the film, weren't up on bricks. This was a common phenomenon among domestic servants in South Africa; whatever the height of the bed, two bricks were invariably placed under each leg. There were many theories as to why, the most common being a superstition. Mere height of the bed wasn't enough. There had to be bricks.

But communication was a problem unless you were an experienced consultant. We told the appropriate person the problem, that the bed should be up on bricks, and when we went back to check later we found that the legs of the bed had been cut right off, and the whole bed now rested on four piles of bricks at each corner. The problem was solved by pulling the bedspread over the side facing the camera, so that only the regulation two bricks would show.

Later the shot was found to be superfluous anyway.

Living in Harare these past twenty years had been a friend from the staff of the *Daily Dispatch* back in East London, Dudley Dickin. Dudley and his wife, Stella, had made the move to what they felt would be a nonracial society sooner than South Africa, and, though the development had taken longer than they had hoped it would, they were now enjoying life in independent Zimbabwe.

Dudley had shown some talent in amateur theatricals in the past, and when Attenborough was looking for someone to play the part of an Afrikaner Nationalist delegate to a party congress I had suggested him. Generally Attenborough disliked working with amateurs, but after a quick audition he had agreed to use Dudley in the scene, which depicted a real incident. In the scene Police Minister Kruger had told delegates to his party's congress that Biko had died following a hunger strike, and a delegate, one Christo Venter of Springs, had stood up and said: "I commend the minister for being so democratic that he gives prisoners the democratic right to starve themselves."

Dudley approached the day of filming the scene apprehensively, but when his moment came he delivered the line in a perfect Afrikaans accent with the right gestures. Having covered such party congresses in South Africa he knew the authentic manner.

Before being involved in the film, he had found out about it in a strange way. He and Stella had been taking their daily walk at sundown in their semirural suburb of Borrowdale when a black Chrysler Valiant had driven by with an East London license plate. Their hometown of East London being more than a thousand miles away, they had been excited at the coincidence. Then a second car had come by, also with an East London license plate, then two with King William's Town plates. The Dickins had thought they were going crazy until they found out these were action cars from the film.

Another coincidence occurred when we began filming in a building in central Harare remodeled to look like the interior of my old newspaper office back in East London. The actress brought out from London to play the part of my secretary was Shelly Borkum, daughter of another old friend from South Africa, Max Borkum.

Max had been president of the Johannesburg Stock Exchange back in 1969 when my *Daily Dispatch* colleagues and I were launching a takeover bid for the country's biggest chain of morning newspapers, and I had been amused when, in putting together a consortium of financiers to participate in the deal, he had said over the phone to one of them: "Well, if you're going to quibble over half a million, forget it!" When the quibbler had reconsidered his petty attitude and unquibbled, Max smiled as he put the phone down and observed: "Money's thicker than blood."

We arrived at the set one morning to see Jason Lehel, the focus puller, garbed in what looked like a Ku Klux Klan sheet, only black, and it was explained that as the camera was doing a tracking shot past a glass partition precautions were being taken against his reflection in the shot. This showed what a problem reflection could be, and that it wasn't only mirrors that had to be checked when shooting. Highly polished furniture could have the same effect.

On occasion, though, the director of photography made use of reflection, particularly in outdoor shots when he wanted to angle the sun's rays a certain way, or throw more indirect light on a scene, or augment the light when the sun wasn't bright enough. For this purpose big reflector screens were pushed into place and tilted to the right angle. They looked like the sails of yachts, and sometimes if they weren't weighted down they tried to take off in the wind.

I became very partial to the reflectors, and would invariably place my canvas chair in the shady side of one of them. This would not only get me close to the action, enabling me to listen for accents without obtruding on eyelines, but would keep the sun off me as well.

The Englishmen were amused at this. But I knew my home continent and remembered how in Central Africa the sun was often more fierce than it seemed to be; that the heat was less noticeable because of the dryness. My frequent resort to the shade of the reflectors later stood me in good stead when I was one of those who didn't succumb to dehydration.

Most of the English members of the unit had a kind of innocence about the sunshine and the heat, and the standbys invariably worked without hats or shirts while performing the most arduous tasks. I had long realized, of course, that the British thrived on extreme discomfort. In fact I had a theory about why the British were so good at middle-distance running and why Sebastian Coe, Steve Cram, and Steve Ovett had dominated the mile run for years. The mile was the optimum race in terms of endurance and speed combined, and was therefore the most uncomfortable. If the mile had to be run while carrying a case full of rocks the British would probably have been even better at it, because as a nation they made a virtue of hardship. You had only to go to one of the major cricket stadiums for an international match to see the extent to which they inconvenienced the spectator—they gave him no parking, poor seating, execrable food, and inadequate scoreboards, which no American sports fan would have tolerated.

No wonder, then, that the Brits scorned the shade of the reflectors and assimilated all the heat of Zimbabwe with a masochistic kind of relish.

One morning near Mutare, while we were filming in the region of the Macheke River, I arrived at the crack of dawn to see an appalling sight. There, perched very high above on a precipitous hillside, was Dickie Attenborough and the whole entourage—camera crew, sound-recording table and all—just because it had occurred to Attenborough that the view from the heights would make a good shot.

I remarked to Norman Spencer: "There's no way I'm mountaineering all the way up there!"

Norman, with irritating conscientiousness, started to scale the heights, dropping the devastating remark: "You should, you know—there's dialogue in this scene."

"Sod the dialogue!" I said, settling down to watch him grasp handfuls of shrub as he hauled himself up the steep slope.

"Dickie will want you up there," he said evilly.

"Sod Dickie too," I said.

Norman ascended further, looking around ostensibly to draw breath but in reality to see if I was feeling guilty.

By now I was. I thought, Damn, this film is important to me, and if they are keen enough to half-kill themselves for the sake of a good camera angle the least I can do is share their aberration. So up I went.

It was, of course, a marvelous view once you were up there, and on the screen it enhanced the scene where Kevin Kline said good-bye to Tami Vundla, played by Tommy Buson, who nearly had a heart attack after making the long climb. Seeing Tommy's physical distress at his age, in his seventies, just to deliver one line, made me feel even guiltier for not having entered more readily into the spirit of artistic insanity.

In the event Attenborough had no queries, only a mischievous gleam in his eye. But if I hadn't made the climb he would probably have thought of something to ask me . . .

Looking down from that height onto the bridge far below, and hearing David Tomblin communicating via walkie-talkie with Clive Stafford on the far side a mile away where he was turning back herds of cows while we filmed, I wondered how filmmakers had managed to communicate at that distance with their runners before the age of two-way radio.

"With flags," said Tomblin through immobile lips. "We had a signaling system—it wasn't all that long ago—but it was much less convenient Clive there are more bloody cattle coming round the corner let's see if we can get rid of them shall we these gadgets are fine while the battery lasts."

One of the strangest experiences for Wendy and me was to meet our five "film children," and to introduce them to our five real children when they came out to spend several weeks watching the shooting.

The three youngest of the film children were all from one family, the Stuart-Walkers, living in Zimbabwe. The smallest was the little girl, whose name was Spring; she played the part of our five-year-old daughter Mary. Her two brothers Hamish and Adam played our two younger sons Gavin and Duncan, who had then been eight and ten years old. When these three met the real Mary, Gavin, and Duncan, they couldn't understand at first why the latter were so much bigger and older than they were, until it was explained that the story they were reenacting had occurred nine years previously.

Our other son, Dillon, who had been thirteen at the time of the escape, was played by fifteen-year-old Graeme Taylor, and our daughter Jane, who had then been fourteen, was played by seventeen-year-old Kate Hardie. Kate had already proved herself a talented actress in films like *Mona Lisa*, in which she had played the very different role of a child prostitute, and she came across well on the screen during the daily rushes. She was the type of actress of whom the professionals said: "The camera loves her," meaning she looked even better on the screen than in real life—a quality apparently shared by many leading film actors.

Graeme Taylor looked the part of Dillon, having the same coloring and sprinkling of freckles across the nose, and his accent was of course perfect because he was a Zimbabwean. Adam Stuart-Walker made an appealing Duncan, but the two who won the hearts of the unit most were little Hamish and his sister Spring. Hamish had cute snaggle teeth and highly mobile eyebrows, and Spring seemed from the first a born actress.

They were, however, a handful on occasion, especially when being filmed for hours in a hot car or being soaked repeatedly by the rain machine in a scene in which they and Penelope Wilton as Wendy had to cross the border into Lesotho in a downpour.

The scene of the kids in the car represented the long drive Wendy had had to make with them while I was heading for the Lesotho border. She had had to pretend, for the watching and listening Security Police, that I was still in the house sleeping late and that she was taking the children to the beach, whereas in fact she was embarking on a four-hundred-mile drive via Umtata to the Lesotho border and our rendezvous. The two older children had known what was happening, but we hadn't risked telling the three smaller ones for fear they might say the wrong thing near one of the surveillance microphones in our house.

The beach balls and toys loaded into the car were as much to deceive them as to deceive the Security Police.

Attenborough decided to shoot this sequence on the strange vehicle known as the "low loader"—the contraption with the wheelless Mercedes mounted on it—with the children inside and Penelope pretending to be driving.

The low loader looked like an eccentric land raft. Very low on the ground, with steel reinforcing to bear the extra weight, it was long enough and wide enough to provide space right around the car "shell" for the camera crew, sound recordist, Attenborough, Tomblin, Nikki Clapp, and a rainmaking device positioned to splash water down onto the front windshield if required. I don't think it was ever required to do so, but it was there in case of need. Pulling all this was a powerful van, or "bakkie" as we call them in South Africa, and the structure itself was on two levels, providing a sort of poop deck on which Attenborough with his straw hat looked as if he were doing a scene from *H.M.S. Pinafore*.

It was a sight to see this thing in full flight, with Penelope and the children inside and Attenborough and his aides around it, the camera pointing into the car interior and Simon Kaye harnessed to the rear ledge or sometimes just balancing there, to monitor over his earphones the quality of sound being picked up by microphones positioned inside the car. We would all set off in convoy behind the low loader, and when we reached a suitable stretch of open highway the rest of us would pull over while it did a series of passes as Attenborough directed the filming operation. Later during rushes we would see and hear the results, with Attenborough's voice providing a constant commentary as he coached the children.

"Adam darling look at Mummy when you say your line. . . . Hamish you mustn't hit Adam dear. . . . Everybody ready? *Uction!* Now look worried everyone . . . worried . . . Adam you left out a word darling the word is Charlie. . . . *Cut it!* . . . You see Adam you're asking Mummy because you're worried about . . . *that's* right . . . well *say* it this time darling now the rest of you remember to look worried. . . . We'll go again. . . . Kate your hair is in your eyes just that strand that's right Graeme keep just in sight of the camera but not so far over and the

ANIMALS,
WHITE
ZIMBABWEANS,
AND
OTHER
DETAILS

rest of you—*Hamish! Stop that!*—now are we all ready? Right—
Uction! Worried now . . . *very* worried . . . *all* very worried . . . David
for some reason we're going too slowly could we have more speed? *Cut
it!* David we're going too slowly, let's have more speed, darlings the
ball has fallen off the window ledge just put it back and the sand bucket
and spade too we'll stop soon for a cool drink are you thirsty? David
can't we get more speed? *More speed?* Penelope darling when you
look around just, like that, yes, now Hamish, Hamish! *Hamish!* Right!
Everybody ready we'll go again David for some reason we're now going too fast . . . that's better now *UGHGHGHGHGHGHGKKK-
SHUNNNNNNNNN!!*"

Sometimes it was a major problem to turn the low loader around
because it was so low that if the road surface wasn't flat the bottom
would scrape, and it was so long and cumbersome that there weren't
many places flat enough and wide enough for the turn. This meant
very long shooting sessions, with the kids getting hot and restless in
the car and Attenborough needing all his reserves of patience, which
seemed limitless.

Attenborough filmed in a variety of hats, but the two most common
were a cap like that of a Dutch barge captain (for cold weather) and
(in hot weather) a wide-brimmed straw hat which looked like a cross
between a Stetson and the headpiece of a Gilbertian jack-tar. A horn-
pipe danced in this would not have been inappropriate, especially on
the poop deck of the low loader.

Those early days of shooting were launched in such harmony and good
humor that I wondered how long the general atmosphere of fun and
friendship would last. I couldn't easily conceive of such a large group
of people, thrown together closely day after day for four months, getting
very far without tensions and hostilities breaking out under the heavy
pressure of work.

Yet that is what happened, and it was largely due to the humor and
relish Attenborough conveyed to the whole unit through his manner
of working. For weeks all I could see was a man whose basic amiability
was consistent and unshakable. Later I came to realize that he was a
far more complex person than that, and that the consistency of his
amiability was occasionally a matter of discipline.

75

At times, for example, he was asked a question when he would rather not have had his concentration disturbed; though his response was always a friendly: "Yes, dear?" and a hand on your arm, the turn from the camera was not as full as it was when you had his undivided solicitude. Such body language took weeks to decipher, because whether or not he was aware of it himself it was as subtle and complex as he was.

His verbal language was far easier to decipher, even when he was speaking in code, and after some weeks it became possible to decode some of the more characteristic Attenborovian phrases according to intonation and inflexion. One of these was: "That's entirely up to you, darling!" This meant: "You'd better bloody do it, or else!"

Another, which meant "I can't believe how stupid you are!" was: "But darling, what I'm *saying* is . . ." An occasional variation to this one was: "But what I *mean* is . . ."

By now I was getting used to the idea of shooting the film out of sequence. Like most people I had imagined films to be shot in narrative sequence, from start to finish, though it was common sense really that this would be a crazy way to do it. The obvious way was to shoot those scenes together which used the same actors and sets, no matter where they fitted in the story.

As it happened, the opening scene of the film was to be shot fairly early in production. Attenborough and Briley had wanted to begin the film with a major scene which set the story indelibly in South Africa and which conveyed the essence of apartheid through a historical fact authentically reenacted. They chose a raid on a squatter township near Cape Town, a raid that had occurred on November 24, 1975.

In fact they could have chosen any one of sixteen such raids that occurred around that period, but the November 24 raid was one of the biggest.

At that time the South African government had decided to crack down much harder than previously on "illegal" blacks in the Western Province—blacks desperate for work who had defied racial zoning to erect shanties and shelters nearer to possible job sources than the remote territories to which the apartheid laws had limited them. By late 1977 these raids had become common knowledge in South Africa, but what most South Africans didn't know was that they had begun two years previously, as our film was about to record.

The raids were appallingly ruthless and callous. Regardless of winter cold the pathetic shelters made up of cardboard, plastic sheeting, scrap wood, and bits of corrugated zinc were smashed down, bulldozed, and burned, along with the meager belongings of the squatters. Sometimes the squatters were alerted to the raid by children placed in strategic positions, who would run through the settlement blowing on whistles to alert the sleeping community (the raids occurred at dawn); those who could would hastily dismantle their shelters and bury the plastic coverings in shallow excavations. But the police got to know of this and started digging up and burning the only coverings the squatters had against the winter rain. The best-known of these camps was Crossroads. The film opens with the start of a raid. A small boy sleeping on a crude platform stirs as the sun begins to rise. He hears the rumble of military vehicles and police trucks, then sees the dust rising from the approaching column. He hurries down from the watching post and runs through the camp blowing his whistle, and people pour from the shelters—but they are too late to escape the raid.

The raiders smash into the camp. Some vehicles drive right into and through the flimsy shelters; others disgorge troops of police. Among the vehicles are the lumbering "hippo" armored trucks with their primeval silhouettes against the morning sky. A Land Rover leads the raid, spewing tear gas from a mounting on its roof, as the police chase after the residents to assault or arrest them. After the initial shock of the raid, bulldozers move in and start leveling the shacks and the rubble is set on fire.

This set was extraordinary in its scope and authenticity. Designed from detailed photographs and with the help of people actually from Crossroads, it was a sprawling shantytown covering several square miles in which actual structures were blended through optical illusion with two-dimensional silhouettes in the distance. The heart of it, where the close-up filming would be done, was an ingeniously built collection of corrugated-iron shacks, makeshift shelters, dusty "streets," improvised "schools," and even a makeshift church with the cross made out of two automobile fenders.

Much of the work had been supervised by a South African, Ian Mulder, who knew Crossroads well and who oversaw construction work during the months in which the set was built, but the guiding spirit in the conception of all the sets in the film was the production designer, Stuart Craig, who was one of Attenborough's most talented associates. He had won an Oscar for production design on *Gandhi*, and by the time we had seen all his sets for our film—of which three were so brilliant that it was a shame they had to be broken up—I heard several of the older hands agreeing that he had surpassed even his *Gandhi* achievements on this one.

To get the effect of dawn Attenborough planned to film the raid sequence at what the unit called the "magic hour"—sunset—and it meant getting the shot done, and done right, within only twenty-five minutes. The sequence had been carefully choreographed and the crowds of extras briefed in the hours leading up to this key period, but the shot could be wrecked by any error involving the scores of police, dogs, and squatters, or by vehicles breaking down or malfunction of the "teargas" machine.

Wendy and I had had a shock on arriving at this set. As we drove into the compound we were confronted with the chilling sight of scores of armed South African police with their trained dogs. Though our reason reassured us that these were film extras it still took a few adrenaline-charged moments to get over the visual impact of those horribly familiar uniforms, and the hairstyles, mustaches, and accents that went with them . . .

I watched Attenborough closely as the time drew near for the crucial shooting, and thought of William Goldman's book, *Adventures in the Screen Trade*, in which he described Attenborough directing a similar scene on an even bigger scale in *A Bridge Too Far*. Goldman wrote that the bridge had been available for only a limited time, that enormous crowds of extras were involved along with several key actors who had to return to America that evening. It had been the only day the scene could be shot, and the only time of day, and if Attenborough "blew it" more than a million dollars would be down the tubes.

According to Goldman, Attenborough had seemed the calmest member of the unit, had reminded some of the extras by megaphone: "Corpses remember to keep your eyes shut!" and had shot the scene as if it had been just another take. Maybe Sir Richard was a better actor behind the camera than in front of it, because the calmness he surely couldn't have felt was as evident when the "magic hour" arrived in Zimbabwe as it appeared to have been in Goldman's account.

There was also the astonishing possibility that the calmness wasn't an act, because as the moment arrived it seemed to me that Attenborough, far from being nervous, was actually relishing the experience and the responsibility. He positively glowed in the setting sun as he passed on a succession of instructions and observations to those around him.

I came to suspect that Sir Richard thrived on adrenaline, and once or twice got the impression that if things went on for too long without a crisis he would be tempted to create one so that he could enjoy dealing with it. There was the occasion when he was encountering trouble over what was known as an "E and O policy" (an insurance policy covering "errors and omissions" in case of lawsuits), without which the film couldn't be made. He had just finished telling me—with an air of devastated concern—how the movie could be wrecked unless this problem was solved at once; then I noticed him immersing himself with equal concern in a long discussion with Lady Attenborough about which wine to have with dinner.

In Briley's story line the raid on the squatter camp was followed by my first meeting with Steve Biko, after Biko's associate, Dr. Ramphele, had marched into my office to complain of an editorial attacking Biko. She had challenged me to meet Biko to test the truth of my accusation that he was an extremist whose Black Consciousness Movement was an overreaction to apartheid amounting to black racism.

The script faithfully followed what had actually happened: I went to meet Biko and was taken by him to Zanempilo, a rural clinic set up by him and his associates as part of their black community program. It was in the course of this first meeting with Biko that I realized he was a man out of the ordinary, and though there was considerable argument and tension at times during that day it was the start of our friendship.

ANIMALS,
WHITE
ZIMBABWEANS,
AND
OTHER
DETAILS

The Zanempilo set created north of Harare was one of Stuart Craig's best. It showed the clinic as it had been in 1976 (by 1986 it had been considerably changed and there were other buildings surrounding it). What the unit had built here was so reminiscent of the original Zanempilo that I walked around nostalgically throughout the week we filmed there. Most of the buildings, like the old church, were insubstantial to the touch, made of plaster and a kind of cardboard in places, but to the eye and on the screen they looked like stone and mortar.

It was at this set that a friend of mine who had known Biko found Denzel Washington's portrayal eerily convincing. His walk and his gestures, and the air of quiet authority Biko had had, seen against the familiar look of the Zanempilo clinic, were uncannily reminiscent of those happier days ten years before.

Approaching the clinic, I was surprised to see round thatched huts such as were in the Eastern province of South Africa—then I realized, as I should have known, that these were also creations of Stuart Craig's. Was nothing real, with that man around? The huts were complete with smoke from cooking fires, and when you looked from close up you realized they were considerably smaller than real huts, for the sake of perspective.

As I walked around, inspecting the complex of buildings at "Zanempilo," I was surprised to see several ostriches in a paddock. Ostriches? There were no ostriches in the region where the real Zanempilo was located—only several hundred miles away in the Karroo. I hated to break the news to the unit because some bright sparks among them (Attenborough and Diana Hawkins included) had thought up the idea to lend a South African touch to the proceedings. It would have been a good idea if we had been filming about the Karroo region . . .

I saw Kevin Kline and Denzel Washington looking through the wire at the ostriches, exchanging views about these strange-looking birds. Dropping their South African accents, they were just two puzzled American guys, and I heard phrases like: "Kinda weird . . ." and "Willya look at that neck . . ."

There was general regret when I said no to the ostriches, though this unit was so determined to be absolutely authentic that after a word with Attenborough David Tomblin merely remarked: "Right—send back the ostriches!" It was one of the stranger sentences I was to hear in the course of shooting.

ANIMALS,
WHITE
ZIMBABWEANS,
AND
OTHER
DETAILS

Outside the fence was tall grass which meant, in that heat, perfect snake country. I noticed the Englishmen blithely stomping around in the thick of it as if snakes didn't exist. The funny thing was that not one snake showed up. If it had, David Tomblin would probably have ordered it to clear the eyeline, and it probably would have obeyed.

In this tall grass of the veld a herd of cattle grazed, and I had assumed they belonged to a local farmer and just happened to be there. I should have known by now that when a film was being shot virtually nothing in the environs was there by chance; in fact the herd was one of David Tomblin's background action effects. As you looked out of the window of the clinic you saw in the distance Stuart Craig's huts with smoke rising from their cooking fires, and, walking past them slowly, David Tomblin's choreographed cattle which had to start moving at a precise point in the dialogue.

Earlier he had had a flock of pigeons flying up out of the grass, having been released at his radio'd call of "Pigeons!" It was after this that I heard his memorable words: "Start the cattle moving!"

One bit of background action at the clinic set didn't go precisely as planned. Actually it was more foreground action than background action. As Denzel Washington was showing Kevin Kline around the grounds of the clinic in a scene in which he was explaining the Black Consciousness philosophy as they walked, Attenborough and Tomblin required one of the extras, playing the part of a patient at the clinic, a very old man, to shuffle slowly across the scene oblivious of the two younger men.

When the old man complied I thought he was overdoing the arthritis act, being bent over nearly double, but when Attenborough called: "Cut!" he didn't straighten up; that was the way he was.

But he wasn't shuffling slowly enough, and though Attenborough repeatedly tried to slow him down the old chap didn't seem able to, and would bolt across the screen like a geriatric Sebastian Coe out of the starting blocks. The amused Attenborough finally gave up and let

81

him go at his own brisk pace—a fact recorded in case anyone seeing the film might think some deep symbolic significance lay behind the alacrity with which the aged man stricken with arthritis zoomed across the yard in the clinic scene.

On the Zanempilo set I first noticed Kevin Kline's habit of turning his face directly into the sun with his eyelids closed before a take, his theory being that this stopped you squinting into the camera. It looked, however, like a mystical rite of obeisance by a sun worshiper.

Kevin had a number of rituals before a scene. He would do relaxing exercises, rolling his neck around on his shoulders while muttering his lines to himself, reaching his arms up to the sky one at a time and sometimes even rolling along his spine a wooden thing like an indented rolling pin to relax his back muscles. Sometimes he'd tune up his vocal chords with what sounded like a series of indignant barks.

He and I played an interminable game of "ghosts," a spelling game in which you take turns adding a letter to either side of a set of letters, losing if your letter spells a word. The trick is that your letter must go toward spelling a real word without completing it. We played for five Zimbabwe dollars a time, payment to be made if one or the other got fifty Zimbucks ahead, but after three months we were exactly level and so declared a draw.

A man of many talents, Kevin often walked off the set after a serious scene pulling a comical face which set us all laughing, especially when he would assume the expression of a half-witted yokel. A perpetual perfectionist, he was frequently self-critical about a scene the rest of us thought had gone very well; often in the daily rushes you would see him on-screen shaking his head or frowning with dissatisfaction after the call of "Cut!" even though his performance had seemed fine to everyone else.

He told me in the beginning that he found it strange to adapt to the Attenborough style of directing, in that other directors he had worked with consulted the actors first about the movements and shaping of a scene before telling the cameraman what to shoot, whereas Attenborough worked out the movements and camera positions with his technicians before discussing them with the actors. But like the other actors he appreciated Attenborough's acting experience as a director, and the fact that Attenborough would give full consideration to any suggestion before shooting a scene, never asking an actor to make a move or speak a line that didn't "feel right" to that actor.

"You can't do it to them, darling," Attenborough told me. "If they don't feel right saying a line, that line won't feel right to the audience—it won't carry the actor's own conviction."

After we had finished filming at the Zanempilo set the site was turned over to the Zimbabwe army for artillery practice, though some of the soldiers, mistaking the date, got in some premature mortar fire before we were quite through. Luckily they scored no direct hits, though they did upset Simon Kaye's sound recording of an off-camera line.

We had done the Zanempilo sequences after a scene filmed at Mbare township, in which Denzel Washington showed Kevin Kline how most black South Africans lived. The stark poverty of Stuart Craig's Mbare set was in sharp contrast to the luxury of the Ridge Road house—as it was meant to be.

At Mbare the local residents had entered so much into the spirit of things and had crowded so close to the actors that the Zimbabwe police had driven them back with brandished whips, sending the crowd into gales of laughter as they retreated. Each retreat lasted barely as long as a take, then they would surge forward excitedly again to be cleared back in time for the next take.

As the shooting went on to well past midnight—in fact we went through until five A.M.—the locals lost their enthusiasm and retired for the night. The cold was so bitter that we huddled close to braziers, except for Ronnie Taylor and his lighting crew who had to keep putting up the appropriate lights and towers. Attenborough was so enveloped within a padded jacket that he looked like the Michelin man.

This was the night I discovered the excellence of the wardrobe department, who lent me one of the war-surplus dlamini greatcoats so loved by black African workmen. Thereafter whenever we filmed in extreme cold I went to borrow my dlamini.

Heading the wardrobe department was John Mollo, another Academy Award–winner on Attenborough's team. One of Britain's leading experts on military uniforms, John was the best-organized man of all when it came to planning his day on the set. Having directed his staff

83

as to the wardrobe requirements, he would bring out a folding chair and table and apply himself to *The Times* crossword or other literary pursuits of an intellectually taxing nature.

The next big scene was shot at the Chibuku Stadium in Harare—a reenactment of the Biko funeral which had been attended by more than fifteen thousand mourners. The Shona extras started arriving in batches from four A.M. This was where Steve Chigorimbo really came into his own, directing the crowds and exhorting them to do what Attenborough wanted until Steve was so hoarse he could barely whisper. When he wanted them to manifest anger he would relate to them parts of their own recent history, leading them in chanting: "Down with apartheid! Down with Botha!" Then they had to be reminded that they were at a simulated funeral, so grinning delightedly was out . . . as was a T-shirt reading SPORT AID 1986.

I didn't count the number of times Steve Chigorimbo called out "*Nyararai!*" ("Quiet!") and "*Mirai!*" ("Keep still!") but it must have run into the hundreds. Yet he never lost his composure or his sunny good humor. In fact the only time I saw him upset to any degree in all our time in Zimbabwe was once on the golf course.

Steve was an even-tempered golfer, though the length of his drive went with a regrettable lack of directional predictability. During our last round there he had finally brought his big drive under control and was hitting all the fairways, heading for his best-ever score, when down the last stretch he hooked his tee shot into the trees.

All we heard from him was a soft and wistful "Damn!" Then he hit a cleanly struck second shot which would have got him out of trouble but for one slender tree which caused the ball to ricochet even deeper into the bush. This time the comment floating back to us was: "Shit!"

Yet again we heard a threshing sound, then again the sound of arboreal obstruction, producing a heartfelt shout which echoed round the course: "*Fuck!*"

By this time his fellow Zimbabweans were laughing so much they could barely stand, and when he emerged from the thickets with thunder on his brow one of them said: "Cut! One more like that, darling!"

This time the phrase hadn't the cadence of Richmond Green . . .

But at the Chibuku Stadium he went for days without hitting any

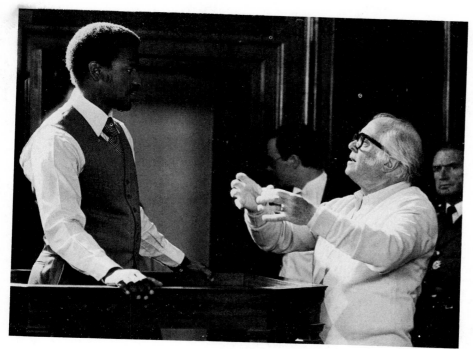

Attenborough coaches Washington for the trial scene.

Washington as Biko during the trial scene.

Wendy Woods *(right)* with Penelope Wilton.

The famous "low loader" with Attenborough amidships.

Opposite, top, Attenborough giving pointers to Penelope Wilton. *(Simon Mein)*

Opposite, bottom, Kline as Donald Woods and John Thaw as Kruger at the Minister of Police's house.

Washington as Biko being restrained by the South African police.

Left to right: Minister of Police Kruger; Colonel Peter Goosen, formerly of the Port Elizabeth Security Police; and Captain Siebert of the Port Elizabeth Security Police. The three men responsible for Steve Biko's death.

Sidney Kentridge,
Biko family lawyer.

Left to right: Doctors Hersh, Tucker, and Lang—the doctors called in by the
Security Police—they chose not to act decisively.

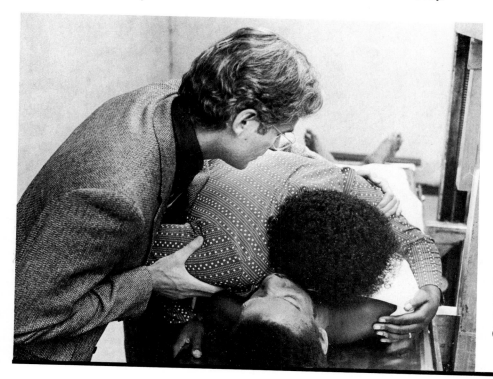

Kline as Woods with
Waterman as Ntsiki
Biko leaning over
the corpse of Biko.
(Simon Mein)

Opposite, top, and above: reenactments of the Biko funeral, involving eighteen thousand Zimbabwean extras. *(Opposite, top by Simon Mein)*

Opposite, bottom, Donald and Wendy Woods, with Steve Chigorimbo between them and Dali Tambo on the left, teach the Shona youths to chant and stamp in the Xhosa way for the reenactment of the Biko funeral.

Biko's widow, Ntsiki, with lawyer Shun Chetty at the inquest, in 1977.

The trials of consultancy—Attenborough asks Woods to choose typical faces for an Afrikaner Nationalist meeting.

The Afrikaner Nationalist meeting from the movie.

metaphorical trees, and his crowd direction contributed considerably to the impact of the Biko funeral scene.

This was the scene the security men had been most worried about in terms of threat to the safety of Attenborough, but he was so involved in overall direction of the scene from a high platform above the crowd that he seemed oblivious to such threat. He was concerned to get the various crowd movements authentically reproduced to accord with the video we had of the Biko funeral.

The scene, in its final version, was a remarkable evocation of the actual Biko funeral, though the magic of cinema had to be pushed to the limit to portray in barely two minutes a funeral that had lasted seven hours. I was interested on the second day of shooting this scene to see that only five thousand of the extras had been retained for the various close-ups and as background for the individual shots. The way they were moved from position to position depending on where the camera pointed showed how five thousand people in an otherwise empty stadium could be moved strategically into camera shot to give the effect of a much bigger crowd once the overall establishing shot was done. Because the audience had already seen a stadium full of people, they would thereafter imagine that segments of crowd they saw were part of the bigger crowd seen earlier. That was the theory, anyway.

Economically, of course, it made sense, because it meant that a scene which took more than two days to shoot would cost far less than it would have cost if all the extras had been retained for the full period. I realized at Chibuku Stadium the extent to which the creative art of cinema was also the creative art of deceit . . . or possibly the art of creative deceit.

Here at Chibuku Stadium I was struck again by the way in which a hundred or so whites could walk into and mingle with a large crowd of blacks in Zimbabwe without tension or incident—something unthinkable in South Africa these days. Even at Steve Biko's real funeral, which had been nearly nine years earlier, there had been tension. Being white South Africans, Wendy and I were conscious of this absence of tension at Chibuku, but I doubt if the Englishmen were. The thought probably never crossed their minds. You could tell by the easy way they were directing the crowd and generally issuing quite peremptory orders at times that they were unaware of any potential edge to the

ANIMALS,
WHITE
ZIMBABWEANS,
AND
OTHER
DETAILS

proceedings. Considering again how comparatively recently there had been a bitter war in Zimbabwe, I thought it remarkable.

For these scenes Attenborough used the new Cobra camera crane which enabled him and the camera crew to ride up high above the crowd and swoop down on parts of it. I had the feeling that, apart from his preoccupation with directing, he was enjoying the ride.

Heights didn't bother him. Once or twice I had to climb up the narrow ladder to the fixed camera tower to discuss a point. He was as much at ease as a steeplejack whereas I, uncomfortable at any height over six feet, had to work at trying to look unconcerned.

The funeral scene in the Chibuku Stadium brought back memories of our maid, Evalina, who had insisted on coming with us to the Biko funeral. The atmosphere had been growing more and more tense as speaker after speaker castigated white arrogance, white racism, white oppression, and white minority rule. There were barely a hundred of us in the huge crowd who were white, and such speeches made us very conscious of our whiteness, especially as angry murmurings and exclamations greeted every attack on white misdeeds.

At the height of this tension Evalina pointed out something to me on the podium. "Look, master . . . ," she began.

"Don't call me master here!" I hissed fearfully.

This exchange had been heard by a sinister-looking black man with a scar down the side of his face, who seemed to be measuring me up for attack. Then he smiled and winked, and I was greatly relieved.

I had said to her again, through lips as immobile as David Tomblin's: "Don't use that word again!"

Fortunately she had barely whispered her reply: "Okay, master."

Evalina had been with us for years and in a variety of ways ruled the household. We had often told her not to call us master and madam but she wouldn't budge from it. Though barely literate, she was shrewd and had a strong personality which she asserted over us all from time to time.

In the film she was played by Sophie Mgcina, a leading South African actress who seemed to understand her character instinctively. In one scene drawn from real life she had been woken up late at night by two policemen who had demanded to see her passbook; Kevin Kline had brandished a pistol at them and made them leave. As Sophie told me: "What no one will realize when they see this scene is that Evalina's shock isn't caused by the two policemen—this sort of thing has often happened to her—but by the sight of her master angry enough to point a gun."

While we were in Harare we managed to get a message through to the real Evalina to arrange for her to come to England when the film was ready for release. Though we had stayed in touch with her, it would be our first reunion in ten years.

On the morning we had set out for the real Biko funeral I had thought it possible, more than possible, that we might not survive the day. A crowd of fifty thousand was expected, and they would be in an angry mood—with their anger directed against *all* whites. If the police were too evident, there could be major trouble.

But we had promised Ntsiki Biko that we would attend, and it seemed unthinkable anyway not to attend Steve Biko's funeral. It would have felt like a betrayal and a surrender to the government.

On the previous evening we had hosted a number of diplomats, journalists, and Progressive members of Parliament such as Helen Suzman, Zac de Beer, and Alex Boraine, who had come to attend the funeral, and all I could tell them was that if the police kept their promise to stay out of sight there was a good chance all would be well. I had, however, sounded more confident about this than I had felt.

Acting as a go-between for Malusi Mpumlwana and the rest of Biko's friends who were planning the funeral, and the uniformed police of the region represented by Brigadier General Smal—a decent man who had contempt for the Security Police—I had arranged a kind of truce for the day. The arrangement was that mourners would be routed directly to the Victoria Ground in King William's Town, provided the police stayed at least two blocks away from the stadium.

Unfortunately the police authorities elsewhere weren't as cooperative as the local police under General Smal, and they had spent the previous night and early morning erecting roadblocks and turning back busloads of mourners—an estimated thirty thousand—from as far afield as Cape Town, Durban, and Johannesburg. As we entered the stadium the more than fifteen thousand present were hearing about this and getting extremely angry.

A serious problem for the fewer than one hundred whites in this vast crowd of angry blacks was the nature and duration of African funerals. They could last up to eight hours, and the number of speakers could go into the dozens—many of them using highly inflammatory language against whites in general. Yet somehow it all worked out and there wasn't any racial violence. It had seemed to me a kind of miracle and I had written about it in my syndicated column.

I hadn't known, and only found out much later, that a white friend of Biko's, Dr. Trudi Thomas, had with her children been surrounded by angry blacks at the edge of the stadium and had been menaced to such an extent that she had hurried away from the funeral.

At various stages the speeches had been so general about what "the whites" had done that I had held my breath, praying for calm to prevail. Fortunately the anger of the crowd had been diverted occasionally by events away from the podium speeches—the chanting entrance of a "guard of honor" of young students, the entry of the funeral cortege, the coffin borne in on an ox-wagon, and the presence of the mourning family had helped to preserve an atmosphere of respect, just when it had seemed that things could get out of hand.

As we reenacted these incidents for the film scene, including the chanting of the students, I had the feeling I had had on a number of occasions during the shooting schedule—that it was a lot more pleasant recalling those tense events through dramatic reconstruction in a safe environment than it had been to live through them at the time. It was a crowd of a very different character and temperament we were dealing with now—Zimbabweans whose war of liberation was over and who, in theory at any rate, no longer had a grudge against whites.

The heat in Harare had made everyone irritable, and to make matters worse the public address system was faulty. At one stage of the last afternoon I had pointed out to Attenborough that some of the actors on the podium should be standing during the singing of the anthem "Nkosi Sikelele iAfrika," and he had replied heatedly that they hadn't been standing during previous setups and that it meant "we couldn't use any of the stuff done during the morning."

Amateur or no amateur, I could see that this was an exaggeration, and put it down to artistic hyperbole. True enough, that particular sequence and setup was nullified, but hardly "any of the stuff done during the morning." I was beginning to realize that at times some of Attenborough's comments fitted Steve Biko's description of African political rhetoric—not always to be taken literally.

Somehow we all, including the huge crowd of extras, survived Attenborough's relentless drive for perfection and finished the sequence to his satisfaction, but I was glad when the funeral scenes were completed, not only because of the security threat they had posed but because it meant we were now finished with the second of the four big crowd scenes in the schedule.

This would have been the best scene for the South African agents to disrupt. All it needed was a tear-gas canister or two in that large crowd to create panic and chaos. The South African government media would have enjoyed reporting: RACE RIOT AT ATTENBOROUGH FILM SET.

ANIMALS, WHITE ZIMBABWEANS, AND OTHER DETAILS

6
CLOSER TO
THE REAL THING

From the stadium we moved to a set in a Harare police station to shoot the scene where Steve Biko was found lying on the floor of his cell with extensive head wounds. Here Wally Schneiderman demonstrated why he was regarded as one of the world's best makeup supervisors, and why he and his daughter, makeup artist Beryl Lerman, made such a formidable team, having done the five-hour daily makeup job on *The Elephant Man*.

For the scenes showing Biko having been assaulted, and later when he was lying dead in the mortuary, they consulted doctors and studied photographs to be sure to get an authentic appearance in the wounds and flesh color. The makeup for Denzel Washington took several hours, and he had to stay in it during lunch. More than one member of the catering staff did a shocked double-take on seeing him in that state.

During this scene occurred one of the quickest bits of construction fakery I saw throughout the production. Attenborough wanted the camera to pull back down a narrow passage, but the brickwork stopped short of the point he wanted to reach. The artists in deceit were summoned. Within a remarkably short time the brickwork appeared to have been extended through to the desired point. It took examination by touch to discover that it wasn't brickwork at all but plasterboard painted to look like brickwork.

Exactly how Steve Biko died was never made known officially. The "inquest" that was eventually held covered up more than it revealed. The government-owned newspaper, *The Citizen*, reported that he had died of renal failure—kidney malfunction—but they didn't reveal that the kidney failure had been due to brain damage. Later, even the government's own officials were unable to dispute pathological evidence that the brain damage had resulted from a number of severe blows to the head.

A clue to what probably happened was revealed when Peter Jones, who had been arrested with Biko, stated to friends on his release more than a year later that during Security Police "interrogation" in Port Elizabeth he had been repeatedly beaten on the head with two sections of hosepipe filled with a heavy substance. One section of hosepipe had been green and the other black, and the Security Police had jokingly referred to them during the beating as "green power" and "black power." It could well have been by this means that Biko was fatally beaten.

Attenborough was determined that we shouldn't invent anything, in the sense of including events we were not sure of—that we shouldn't have a scene showing Biko actually being beaten as we had no exact knowledge of the details. We knew he had been beaten, but not how or by how many attackers. Attenborough's attachment to fact wasn't due only to love of truth, but also to practical cinematic sense; he reasoned that if even one material inaccuracy could be challenged successfully, it would call into question the veracity of the rest of the film. We therefore reenacted only what we knew for certain: that Biko was taken handcuffed into the cell, and that he was later found lying on the cell floor in the condition shown; and what the doctor and Security Police colonel said according to their inquest evidence.

Filming in these police cells was a depressing business because the atmosphere was so authentic—these were real cells—and we were all glad to finish with the place and get back to outdoor scenes.

As with Kevin Kline, I was deeply impressed by Denzel Washington's professionalism. He was so steeped in the part and the scene that throughout the period we filmed in the police cells he hardly communicated with anyone, even off the set.

On the first day he went before the cameras I had been asked to help "choreograph" a rugby movement in which he had to receive a pass, break two tackles, and fall on a precise mark on the ground. Though he had never handled a rugby ball he had played American football, and he did precisely what was required, every time. Eleven times he landed on that mark in exactly the right position. But during one take an opposing player had landed on Washington the wrong way and he twisted his ankle. Gone suddenly was his African accent, and you couldn't have heard anything more American than his sharp cry of "Oh shheeeyitt, man!"

His most powerful performance, not only in terms of the effect of it on film but its effect on all of us who watched the scene being shot, was the scene showing Biko being arrested at a police roadblock. Washington managed wordlessly, somehow by expressing his thoughts through his eyes, to convey that he knew this was it—probably the end of his career as a dissident and possibly the end of his life—and as he climbed slowly out of the car to produce his identity pass to the police officer there was such controlled power in his acting that I felt the impact of it. I looked around at the others watching this scene and the power of it showed on their faces. Attenborough was visibly moved.

Peter Jones had later told friends that the Security Police at the roadblock had obviously had no idea who was in the car, and could hardly believe it when they discovered Biko's identity. A number of cars ahead of them had been given a perfunctory check, but a defective boot lock on the trunk of their car had attracted the notice of the policemen, who had been talking among themselves of "calling it a night" and dismantling the roadblock.

After they were arrested and transferred to Port Elizabeth, Biko and Jones were separated. That was the last time Jones saw Biko.

This roadblock scene was shot late at night in bitter cold. It was the night I saw Nikki Clapp typing in her continuity sheets by the light of her special spectacles, so that she looked like a visitor from Mars. That night we barely finished shooting in time to beat the dawn, and Simon Kaye had some problems doing wild-track recordings unspoiled by cockcrow.

For the scenes in which Biko was subjected to cross-examination in the SASO (South African Students Organisation) trial of 1976—a trial in which members of the Black Consciousness–oriented SASO were accused of inciting blacks to hate whites—we used the buildings of the High Court of Harare, and those two scenes, which were to be flashbacks in the film, took three days. Ian Richardson was so convincing as the conservative South African prosecutor that one of the right-wing white Zimbabwean extras playing lawyers assumed these were his real political views, and sidled up to him out of earshot of Attenborough to whisper solidarity and encouragement.

This caused Ian a blend of chagrin on principle and professional satisfaction on the issue of performance credibility. The chagrin had outweighed the satisfaction, but for the sake of the production he had reined in his irritation until the scene was safely shot before expressing himself tersely to the man concerned.

Michael Turner, who played the judge, couldn't have been bettered in the role. Born in South Africa, he knew just how far to take accent and intonation without sending it up, and I enjoyed his line, repeated dozens of times for the various angles and close-ups: "But why dew yew call yourselves black? I mean, yew people are more brrown than black . . ." Which had called forth Biko's memorable reply: "Why do you call yourselves white? You people are more pink than white."

Michael, one of Britain's favorite cads as the ruthless magnate J. Henry Pollard in the popular soap opera *Crossroads*, was, like Ian Richardson, one of the leading actors ready to come all the way to Zimbabwe just for a few lines, because of the theme of the film and because of their personal regard for Attenborough.

In the real SASO trial, in which nine young blacks were sentenced to several years on Robben Island political prison for promoting the Black Consciousness philosophy, the judge's attractive daughter attended the proceedings as a spectator. So did the brother of one of the nine accused. He and the judge's daughter fell in love and ran away to London to get married, since the apartheid laws made interracial marriage a crime in South Africa. We felt it was a pity we didn't have the film time to include this cameo.

For this trial Steve Biko was given permission to travel unescorted to Johannesburg, and he made use of the rare dispensation to pay us a visit at our house "on his way." It had amused us to speculate on how he would justify a deviation to East London as being on his way—Johannesburg being in the opposite direction—but that was how he often played things, pushing opportunities to the limit.

After his death, when I was writing the biography *Biko*, Wendy went to Johannesburg to photocopy the transcript of his evidence for me, as I wasn't allowed to travel. When she was handed a pile of typed pages ten inches high she said she didn't want the transcript of the whole trial, only the Biko evidence; the reply was that the ten-inch pile *was* the Biko evidence . . . The evidence of the full SASO trial made a pile of transcript several feet high.

For the purpose of our film the SASO trial was featured mainly to demonstrate the intellectual power of Steve Biko—his skill and articulateness under cross-examination and his political depth under public challenge. In fact the main significance of the real SASO trial was that nine young blacks were prosecuted for their attitudes rather than their actions. Officially they were accused of inciting blacks to hate whites—an irony in view of the fact that the South African government in every election campaign had incited whites to fear and, by implication, to hate blacks. But what was really on trial in this case was the presumption of blacks in daring to think like people free to be themselves.

Shortly after we finished the courtroom scene the unit had to leave Harare to film in other parts of the country as Zimbabwe was due to play host to more than a hundred delegations of the Non-Aligned movement and hotel bookings were severely limited. The move had been planned many months beforehand; the unit had known well in advance about the conference and had arranged the shooting schedules to get us to locations away from Harare during that time.

Hotel bookings were so limited in the capital during the conference of Non-Aligned states that a number of Zimbabweans, white and black, offered their homes to delegates free of charge. However, some of the wealthy whites with fine houses in Harare were renting them out to visiting heads of state at considerable profit. One white millionaire Zimbabwean rented his house out to Dr. Fidel Castro of Cuba. He was Ian Smith, formerly prime minister of Rhodesia and lifetime scourge of Marxists.

As Max Borkum would have said: "Money's thicker than blood."

The position of Ian Smith in black-ruled Zimbabwe was of special interest to me. As a journalist I had met him in the days when he was prime minister of Rhodesia.

It had been his habit from time to time to take a vacation cruise along the South African coast, putting in at Durban, East London, Port Elizabeth, and Cape Town, and while the liner was berthed in East London harbor a copy of the *Daily Dispatch* was pushed under his cabin door. It happened to contain a strongly worded anti-Smith and anti-"Rhodesia" editorial, and he was so shocked that I was "so misinformed" about his policies that he telephoned to invite me aboard for a discussion.

It was a tedious talk, because although his vocabulary wasn't the blunt vocabulary of apartheid, his sentiments were obviously that way inclined; his policies were, if not apartheid in full, certainly so closely related as made no matter. Smith had a humorless manner and was not articulate.

When his kind used to speak of standards being lowered under black rule, they meant white standards, of course. To black children now able to attend good schools for the first time standards are being raised, and the common denominator is inevitably to be higher for the majority under black rule.

The then South African prime minister, Vorster, had no high opinion of Smith's intelligence. As a newspaper editor I used to have an annual discussion with Vorster which, he said, was to enable him to find out what "the enemy" was thinking; when Smith declined the offer of a deal which, in effect, would have meant majority rule after fifteen more years of white minority rule (Smith saying he wanted a thousand years!), Vorster commented drily: "Dit laat my dink aan die storie van die Sultaan se perd" ("It reminds me of the story of the Sultan's horse").

There was, said Vorster, a certain Sultan who offered pardon to two thieves condemned to death, if either of them could teach his horse to talk. The first thief admitted he couldn't teach a horse to talk, and was summarily sentenced to be taken away and beheaded. But before being dragged away he heard the Sultan pardoning the other thief, and he asked the other thief how he had replied to gain the pardon. The other thief said he had replied: "Mighty one, I can indeed teach thy horse to speak, but it takes three years." Vorster gave a wintry smile and said: "Smith should have taken his fifteen years."

It would certainly have been longer than the time he had left for white minority rule in Rhodesia, which was less than half that, and a lot less than a thousand years . . .

The extraordinary thing about this insight of Vorster's, of course, was that he could see the inevitability for Rhodesia but not for South Africa. He couldn't apply his reasoning to himself.

In Zimbabwe I was interested to see that although Ian Smith had been responsible for sending many young whites to their deaths in a hopeless cause, and although one saw numbers of young whites maimed, without arms or eyesight, there seemed little personal bitterness among them toward Smith. Many of the whites who had stayed on in Zimbabwe did regard him as an old fool who had misled them, but some of the war veterans were strangely tolerant of his failure to keep his promises of certain victory.

Even more amazing was the tolerance toward him by black Zimbabweans who had fought against his army and won. As we drove past Smith's multimillion-dollar cattle ranch near Shurugwi I asked Steve Chigorimbo why a local high school was still named after Smith's family. "Well, it *is* part of our history, you know," said Steve. "The whiteys lost—that doesn't mean we want to take everything from them. That old man now, he can't do us any more harm. Let him keep his damn farm and his fancy house."

Some of the black Zimbabweans qualified their resentment of Smith by saying: "At least the old bastard stayed on here. He's now a Zimbabwean!"

Wendy flew back to London with the children as the time came for the unit to leave Harare to the Non-Aligned conference, and would rejoin us after a month when we returned from filming in other parts of the country. It had been good to see the children relishing the Southern African climate again; they had enjoyed their stay with the unit.

They had been interviewed for a television documentary about the making of the film. Jo Wright, director of the documentary, had told us their answers had been "forthright" and "interesting"—two adjectives which caused Wendy and me some trepidation, wondering how frank they had been about parental and family matters usually kept within the house . . .

What the hell, we thought. Let it all hang out. Well, almost all . . . We certainly weren't going to inquire further or attempt any parental censorship, no sir. Still, we did wonder what each of the five had said, and looked forward with mixed feelings to seeing the documentary to find out . . .

The rest of us left in convoy for a succession of locations in Zimbabwe—Gweru, Shurugwi, Bulawayo, Mutare, and Macheke River. For most of the members of the unit it would be the first chance to see the beauty of the Zimbabwe countryside, in particular the eastern highlands where we were to spend two weeks shooting.

Several of these towns now had new names, or rather had had their original names restored to them after white rule had ended. Under the whites these towns had had names like Gwelo (now Gweru), Selukwe (Shurugwi), Umtali (Mutare), and Fort Victoria (Masvingo). I remembered having had an argument with Wendy's right-wing Uncle Doug in Bulawayo fourteen years previously. Doug Preston had been so right-wing that he had thought Ian Smith was practically a Communist.

"There'll always be white rule here! Even if we all retreat to Salisbury we'll fight it out!" he had thundered. More in irritation than prescience I had countered: "There'll *be* no Salisbury, Doug. When the blacks take over they'll give it the name of that black township there—Harare!"

Unfortunately he hadn't lived to see that prediction fulfilled.

Actually such predictions weren't all that difficult to get right. In postapartheid South Africa such cities as Johannesburg, Pretoria, Durban, Cape Town, Kimberley, Port Elizabeth, and East London would probably be renamed Mandela, Tambo, Luthuli, Sisulu, Sobukwe, Mbeki, and Biko.

When we reached Gweru I noticed that Stuart Craig had put up signs reading "Greatermans" and "Komga"—Greatermans being a local department store and Komga being a neighboring town—to provide an authentic touch of East London for the scene in which Penelope was to drop Kevin on the outskirts of the city to begin the reenactment of my hitchhike in disguise to the Lesotho border.

Here I had something of a shock, because I saw a truckload of black soldiers driving by in South African uniform. There had been a misunderstanding with Jack Briley somewhere along the line, because when the script was consulted there it was prescribed—black soldiers. It was also on the day's callsheet.

"No way," I told Attenborough. "No such thing as black soldiers armed with guns in South Africa."

He pointed out that I should have spotted this anomaly before, and I acknowledged the fact. "So it would be inaccurate if we showed such a scene reflecting 1977 in South Africa?" he said.

"It certainly would," I said.

Out came the black soldiers, to be replaced by white soldiers, and I resolved to read the callsheet more closely thereafter. This would have been a worse gaffe than showing ostriches being farmed near King William's Town . . .

It was in Gweru that I began noticing the strangely old-fashioned style in which some members of the unit spoke of and to women. The actresses were called "sweetheart" just like in the Humphrey Bogart movies of the thirties, and actresses like Wabei Siyolwe and Josette Simon were referred to as "little Wabei" and "little Josette" although they were bigger than some of the men in the unit. I wondered if this was because the self-absorbed world of moviemaking had alienated some of them from the real world and its newer sensitivities. Certainly their assumption of control over their surroundings bordered at times on arrogance, and several of them were quick to pass judgments on the ways of nonprofessionals.

David Tomblin, for example, disapproved of having canvas chairs near the filming and said that if he had his way chairs would be banned from the set. I decided that if I were a magistrate and David appeared before me for sentencing I would condemn him to four months of having to stand watching me edit a newspaper—writing each headline eleven times over.

Most of us were accommodated at the quaint old Midlands Hotel in Gweru, a colonnaded reminder of Victorian grandeur in the colonies. The high ceilings and broad verandah recalled that age of gentility, but didn't quite go with the nightly high jinks of the local inhabitants in the bar, fueled by that most recognizable African preference—whether in Nigeria or South Africa—for quart bottles of beer rather than puny little pint bottles which no African lager drinker could take seriously.

Watching the scene of Kevin being dropped by Penelope to start the hitchhike reminded me of another true incident Jack Briley had left out of the script—in this case because of the time factor. Several such incidents could have been included but would have made the film too long.

During my escape, I was disguised as a priest. I took a prayer book with me as a "prop." As I was about to leave the house, Wendy checked through it to see if there was anything in it likely to identify me. There was: written on the first flyleaf was my name, followed by the date of my First Communion. Some disguise . . . She tore out the page and handed the missal back.

If we had put that incident in the film a lot of people would have regarded it as an extra touch included to hype the story up. In fact, there was yet another true touch to the story that wasn't included for the same reason, and it was on the same scale of drama as the police searchlight at the border and the prayer-book inscription. It happened after Wendy and the children had left the house, ostensibly to go to the beach, but in reality to drive to her parents' house in Umtata one hundred fifty miles from East London. The plan was that they would wait there until ten A.M. for a phone call I would make at that time from Maseru—if I got through. Unforeseen delays kept me far behind schedule in getting across the border, and it was only a reckless feat of driving by my Australian friend Bruce that got me to Maseru literally a few minutes before ten A.M.

That ten A.M. phone call was vital, because the arrangement was that if the call didn't come through Wendy was to assume I'd been caught and go back home immediately with the children to avoid being implicated in my attempted escape.

But the journey of Wendy and the kids to Umtata had also not gone smoothly. Our Mercedes, which was fairly new and had never given any kind of trouble, developed a distributor fault. As a result, about halfway to their destination the car slowed down and had barely any power on the uphills—of which there are many on the road to Umtata. In consequence they barely made it to Umtata in time for the call. A journey which should have got them there more than an hour earlier, round about 8:30 A.M., got them there only moments before I made the call.

Again, if Briley had put that into the script it would have looked too much of a coincidence to be credible on-screen. Clearly there were more coincidences in real life than in the movies . . .

In Gweru we also filmed a sequence that had an allegorical basis. There was no cinematic way of showing satisfactorily how Steve Biko had circumvented his banning restrictions to communicate with many thousands of blacks through a column in my newspaper under another name, so Attenborough had hit on the idea of a scene showing Biko, while hidden in the crowd, addressing spectators at a soccer game. This scene, which involved many angles and close-ups, took two days to film. When we saw the rushes we realized the device had worked.

In the scene Attenborough conveyed the power of Biko's logic by preceding his speech with a rabble-rousing introduction by a demagogue, and had the young soccer players one by one pausing in their pregame kickabout to listen to the more thoughtful and reasoned Biko arguments. The demagogue was excellently played by Alton Kumalo, one of South Africa's leading actors, and the contrast in style between the two speeches conveyed exactly what Attenborough was after.

We moved to Shurugwi to film a scene showing Kevin Kline reenacting my hitchhike through the town of Stutterheim on New Year's Eve on my way to the Lesotho border. I was haunted by the old hotel we used for the New Year's revelers. Shurugwi was about the same size as the small town of Stutterheim, and the Grand Hotel was exactly the sort of hotel to be found in Stutterheim.

The hotel had been closed for over a year, and I wandered through its big rooms and its derelict ballroom, and along its long balconies, imagining the style it had represented in the past. This had been Ian Smith's turf; indeed he still lived on his ranch a few miles away, and I could imagine the ballroom echoing to applause for speeches such as he had been delivering so confidently only a few short years before, and of which recent history had made such nonsense.

It was sad to reflect that such a lesson was still to be undergone by my own country when its turn came, and that President Botha was still talking the sort of talk Smith had been talking seven years before in that Shurugwi ballroom.

Now the pretensions of the place were pathetically stripped away, the paint peeling from the high walls and handsome door frames through which elegant women and men in dinner clothes had passed full of foolish confidence that they could hold onto what they had in such abundance.

Shurugwi had been the playtown of rich gold miners. Many of the gold mines in the time of "Rhodesia" had been family mines, and a school friend had taken me to one which was his home. It had been a beautiful place with a luxurious house; the privately owned gold mines around Shurugwi must have been like it. But now most of them were mined out, and the families had moved on because of this or because of the war, so that little was left of the lifestyle of the town but the buildings like the abandoned Grand Hotel.

At the end of the long ballroom was a stage that had served as the bandstand, and one could guess the numbers they must have played, in a style then regarded as the very latest. Here, too, was a reminder of the aspirations white minorities had had to recreate the style of Europe in Africa. This was the sort of ballroom you would have seen in Eastbourne or Brighton. The once beautiful ceiling, arched and ornamental, had been defaced with a coat of paint in a hideous blue, obviously by one of the last in the line of increasingly desperate proprietors. But it had been a last fling before the inevitable realization that the Grand would never again have the volume or affluence of custom to justify so many rooms and so much space.

Up on the balconies I walked in the semidark, looking down on the unit as they stood in knots preparing to shoot. David Tomblin was coaching a crowd of extras dressed in evening gowns and tuxedoes about how to cross the street toward the brightly lit hotel, calling "Happy New Year" as the crowd within sang: "Should auld Acquaintance be forgot . . ."

The hotel had been brought to life again for midnight. There was dancing, there were streamers and firecrackers, multicolored lights, and couples crossing in silhouette behind the windows as directed by Roy Button and Patrick Kinney. The scene showed cars pulling up, friends greeting each other in a celebratory mood, and the chorus striking up—while over on the corner diagonally opposite, Kevin Kline, dressed as a priest, was about to be picked up by a police patrol car.

This pickup represented several scares I had had the evening I passed through Stutterheim—not counting the searchlight on the border.

Once I had had to dive into a roadside ditch when a car had swept around a corner unexpectedly. The ditch had been several inches deep in water.

Later I had noticed two police cars hemming in the car I was riding in—one in front and one behind—and they had kept this formation for several miles before moving on.

Then the car I was in had had a puncture, attracting helpers in other cars.

In the village of Jamestown a police van had pulled up alongside at a traffic light, and the police driver had appeared to be looking intently at me (when you're in disguise you often forget you're in disguise) before turning away.

While it was true that I had been given a lift by police at some stage of the journey, it hadn't happened exactly as Jack Briley had written the scene; but I understood that his crafting of it made it a dramatic synthesis of several experiences I had had that night, so I had no problem with the scene as I saw it being lit on that street corner in Shurugwi. On this corner Attenborough and Ronnie Taylor were now conferring about the lighting and the camera angles. I left the sad upper floor of the hotel with all its ghosts and went to rejoin the living.

A nearby garage had had a supply of liquor brought along by some of the white extras, and only a few moments of conversation with them revealed that an unrepentance about "Rhodesia" had been brought to the surface by the booze. One of them said aggressively: "They'll tell you this is Shurugwi, but I'm telling you it's Selukwe and it'll stay that way!" One of his tuxedo jacket sleeves was empty; he had lost an arm in the war.

I mentioned how on my last visit to Rhodesia I had been told by people like him that the "ters" could never win, yet here were the "ters" (terrorists) running the country without cutting the throats of the whites or roasting white babies. But I don't think he heard me properly—he was too busy ascribing the troubles of "Rhodesia" to the perfidious British, like Harold Wilson, who had "left them in the lurch."

It was pointless to dispute the matter. In fact Prime Minister Harold Wilson had leaned so far over backward to help the whites—even so far as to turn a blind eye to oil supply—that in my opinion he had not been far short of Ian Smith's degree of culpability for all the needless bloodshed there had been in "Rhodesia."

Some of these white Zimbabweans, who owned nearby premises, would not at first let black members of the unit use the toilet. But Steve Chigorimbo reasoned with them, and they relented.

Steve was aware of the little nest of inebriated "Rhodesians," and I marveled at his restraint. One telephone call from him and they could have been in serious trouble, but he just winked and said: "Yesterday's people. We leave them alone and they either become Zimbabweans or leave. You must think of all the good whites who have stayed and forgotten the past."

I thought the unrepentant revelers had inherited better "terrorists" than they deserved.

I thought also of one of the most pathetic of all the recorded deathbed sayings in history: when Cecil Rhodes turned to his secretary and said hesitantly, "They . . . they don't change the names of countries, do they?" It was as well for his peace of mind that more than a half century would elapse before Northern Rhodesia became Zambia and Southern Rhodesia became Zimbabwe.

7
LEAVING ZIMBABWE

The unit moved to Bulawayo—or rather elements of it did while others went on to prepare for shooting in Mutare—to film the reenactment of the Soweto demonstrations of 1976. The "second unit," having distinguished itself in much of the work on the Crossroads scene earlier, had been busy for some time in preparation for these powerful crowd scenes.

The second unit was headed by Peter MacDonald as director/cameraman—a man who relied a lot on flair and produced visually beautiful scenes which had strong impact. He had been camera operator on a number of Attenborough films. Not as strict as Attenborough in the detailed choreography of a crowd scene, nor as precise in his direction of actors, MacDonald achieved his effects with a kind of spontaneity I had first noticed in the rugby scene with Denzel Washington. He tended to give a broad outline and then sort of "let it happen." In the Soweto scene this was effective in several respects.

Attenborough joined him in Bulawayo and I noted that, while he made many suggestions, he was careful not to "take over" from MacDonald in the scenes they had previously planned together. I was also interested to see that in the big scene where the Soweto schoolchildren confronted the armed police both MacDonald and Attenborough were actually operating cameras.

I asked Sheila Attenborough what the cinematic technicians' union would have to say about "Dickie" operating a camera, but she said he was a member of the union and had had his ticket for many years.

There wasn't much shade in Bulawayo, and the high temperature wasn't always due only to the sun. Some of the volatile young Ndebele youths storming the "police" and hurling fake "bricks" and "stones" were not as laid back as the Shona in Harare, and once or twice they entered into the spirit of the thing too convincingly. When some of them ran out of fake stones they picked up and used real ones.

For their part some of the young Bulawayo whites dressed as police and army had recently been in a real war and displayed chilling familiarity with the automatic rifles, not always having to be shown how to deploy for firing and the like. One of them, referring to the too-lively blacks in tones more fitting to six years previously, said in effect that if they wanted to make this thing real, he and his mates would do the bloody same.

This was all very well and good for the movie, in that the hostility between the two sides was looking realistic; but while this added to the impact of the scene the last thing we wanted was for our film dedicated to racial harmony to create the opposite! Some soothing words were spoken on both sides, all non-fake bricks and stones were removed from the scene, and the truce prevailed.

The property department, or "props," could have a crucial effect on the look of a film. Working in conjunction with "special effects" and "stunts," they could pull off in safety what would otherwise have been dangerous or foolhardy. Many tourists who did the Universal Studios tour through the years saw how bottles could be structured to "break" in a certain way, or chairs to splinter in a barroom brawl. This had often been overdone in Westerns, in which balcony balustrades and stair-banisters had appeared ludicrously easy to break under impact, but in a quality film these departments were usually concerned with more mundane incidents than brawls. Yet some of the film stunts in Zimbabwe were as taxing as these.

The stunt coordinator, Peter Brace, spent a lot of time teaching extras how to fall when shot, or when tumbling off the back of a truck. The special effects department was required to see to such things as bullets appearing to hit the ground (they used small charges buried in the earth) and bullet wounds.

The Soweto sequence was to be the last major crowd scene in the film, introduced by a flashback of Biko phoning Woods to say: "Have you heard about Soweto?" Steve Biko had been excited that day and I, conscious that our phone conversation was being monitored, had responded with a nervously neutral sound in my throat. This had amused Biko a great deal.

As subsequent events showed, Soweto 1976 was the turning point in black resistance in South Africa, and the country's townships have never been tamed since.

The best bit of cinematic deception I saw in the Soweto sequences was when one of the schoolboys, chased by armed police, had jumped up to get over a "barbed-wire fence," at which blood appeared to issue from his fingers; then he slumped against the fence, "shot." I walked over to the place after the scene was shot and found that the vicious-looking barbed wire had been silver-colored plastic and that the "blood" came from a sac of fluid held in his hand.

I was told that most of the people in "props" or "stunts" or "special effects" were people who had started as general workers on film sets, as rookies with no special experience. One young member of the unit had literally pestered his way onto it. Chris O'Hare, a Missourian from Kansas City, had been attending Britain's National Film School; from the moment he heard of the production he began to write applying for a job, any job, on it. When his letters and phone calls were to no avail, he wangled an appointment with Terry Clegg ostensibly on another matter. As Attenborough was a founding governor of the school and always tried to have at least one trainee from it on his films, he and Terry Clegg decided to reward the imaginative persistence of Chris O'Hare by taking him onto the unit. They were to have no regrets, because Chris soon proved to be one of those who could be relied on to do what was necessary in a variety of capacities, and if he didn't know how, he learned quickly. He was, in short, a "can-do" person.

One of the reasons I like America is because it is essentially a "can-do" country. Present most functionaries in the United States with a problem, and whether they are telephone operators or hotel receptionists or whatever, the usual reaction is the word: "Okaaaaaaay . . ." It is drawn out, with an upward inflection, and means: "I may not immediately know how to handle this, and I may be stalling till I find out, but I am certainly disposed to finding out." And invariably they do.

Another young man who had a unique position in the unit was listed, for security reasons, as "Daley Campbell"; his function, purposely vague, was given as "African liaison." This might have seemed strange to anyone talking on the phone with him, because his accent was that of an English public school with the assured drawl of Eton and Harrow. In fact he was the son of one of the two men most hated by the South African government; in the event of a successful revolution in South Africa at that time "Daley's" father would almost certainly have become prime minister or president, with his ex–law partner Nelson Mandela having first choice of these two offices.

"Daley" was Dali Tambo, son of Oliver Tambo, the president-general of the African National Congress of South Africa. Dali was on the unit mainly because of his expertise in two areas. Soweto '76 had been the subject of his degree thesis, and he was an adviser on cultural matters with special reference to African songs.

Wendy's father, Harold Bruce, had had a construction company in the Transkei Territory which had built a power station near Umtata. This installation was blown up by the ANC during a week in which I had tea with Dali Tambo and his mother in London. That same evening I dined with Harold and Kay Bruce, and I considered it an unusual experience to have been, on the same day, with people whose associates had built a power station and people whose associates had blown it up.

The South African situation produced a number of such contradictions. I once also met within two days: (a) an old friend, Laurence Baillie, who told me his son had been called up for military service on the borders against the insurgents; and (b) a black exile whose son was at an ANC military training camp in Tanzania. It was possible that the sons of my two friends would soon be trying to kill each other.

I flew to Mutare with Diana Hawkins and the second unit still photographer, Simon Mein, in a small aircraft which Jack Briley would have described as "rinky-dink" . . . but sometimes the rinky-dinks gave you a better view of the countryside, and the Zimbabwe countryside looked increasingly beautiful the further east we flew.

One of the first scenes we filmed in Mutare was my arrival in Maseru, Lesotho, after my escape from South Africa. Kevin Kline had to reenact my run from the car, driven by my friend Bruce, to the office of the British High Commission, where I was to make the all-important ten A.M. call to Wendy at Umtata.

After he had done the first take Kevin asked me: "Was that how it was?"

"Yes," I said, "but you run too athletically—I have an awkward, clumsy run."

Kevin looked mortified. "But I specially made it clumsy and awkward! You thought *that* wuz *athletic*?"

John Hargreaves was playing the part of Bruce, who had met me on the Lesotho side of Telle Bridge and had driven me at breakneck speed to Maseru so that I could make the crucial telephone call. The real Bruce was Bruce Haigh, an Australian diplomat. Jack Briley had turned him into a journalist for script purposes, one of the reasons being that the screen Bruce had been based on two people, and it would not have been fair to Bruce Haigh's diplomatic career to portray him planning my escape as well as meeting me at the border.

Bruce had been one of the most successful diplomats to serve in South Africa. As second secretary at the Australian embassy in Pretoria, he was one of the few diplomats who took the trouble to meet real black leaders like Steve Biko. (At his request I had arranged a meeting, and Steve and his associates had grown to like and trust him.) Bruce also got to know members of the banned African National Congress and Pan Africanist Congress. Not only was he able to file more accurate reports of the South African situation than other diplomats; he was also able to get scholarship and aid grants from Australia for black educational and welfare projects in South Africa.

For these reasons, and possibly because he helped me get from Telle Bridge to Maseru, the South African government demanded that Canberra withdraw him. To its credit the Australian government stood firm and Bruce served out his term. He returned to Canberra in due course, was promoted, and served in the Australian embassy in Saudi Arabia before being sent as first secretary to the Australian embassy in Pakistan.

During his stay in South Africa Bruce had been subjected to a vicious smear campaign similar to the one against the Attenboroughs during their visit, though in a different style. Because Bruce had gone to visit Dr. Ramphele in her place of banishment near Tzaneen, and had stayed overnight in that remote place, the Afrikaans newspapers reported that he had been seen in her house in pajamas—their implication being that he was therefore having an affair with her. Bruce responded with a mixture of amusement and indignation: "I've never worn pajamas in my life!"

John Hargreaves portrayed the character of Bruce authentically. He even laughed exactly like him—unless there is an Australian national laugh—and showed why he is one of the most highly regarded actors from Australia. He told us some Australian friends had suspected our film was a send-up of Australians, as they had heard the character he was playing was called Bruce! John was able to assure them that our Aussie was indeed called Bruce, and had so been christened.

The worst scene to watch throughout our filming in Zimbabwe was the scene we shot in Mutare to reenact the day Ntsiki Biko and I went to a mortuary in King William's Town to see the body of Steve Biko.

Ntsiki and I had been given the runaround that day and had succeeded in gaining entry into the mortuary only by sheer persistence. Once inside we saw Steve's body, appallingly different from what he had looked like alive.

Briley had stuck close to the real event in writing the scene and watching Kevin Kline and Juanita Waterman, with Ken, the newspaper's photographer, entering the room in which the body was kept, was horribly reminiscent of the real event.

Stuart Craig had managed to find a building in Mutare, normally a gymnasium, which could be made to look like the mortuary. Attenborough immediately approved it, thinking it would be particularly suitable, and when all the adaptations were complete it was uncannily like the real thing. The outside was shabby, the inside sordid, and the room in which the corpses were kept was exactly like the room in King William's Town, complete with the sliding "trays" which held the bodies.

I remembered that day well. On seeing Biko's body I had been hesitant to fold back the sheet that covered it, but I had been so conscious of the need to record every mark of injury that I had inspected the body minutely, especially the head. Any feelings of revulsion at seeing a mutilated corpse were so outweighed by anger at what they had done to him that I was able to make a close observation of his injuries.

Anger had therefore been the predominant emotion for me that day, and when the scene was shot in Mutare I felt it all surging back.

Attenborough spent an extra-long time with the actors before this scene, and between his motivational suggestions and their artistic receptivity to him they combined to give what I thought were peerless performances. Juanita Waterman in her expression and bearing looked and did exactly as Ntsiki had looked and done that day. She had the same calm strength, assailed but undominated by grief, and as I watched I felt she bore a particularly strong physical resemblance to Ntsiki. Kevin Kline also had extraordinary intuition that day, because his facial expression and bearing exactly recaptured how I had felt and reacted.

What made it all the more poignant was that Wally Schneiderman and Beryl Lerman had made Denzel Washington's "corpse" look exactly as Steve Biko's had looked, especially with regard to the facial injuries I had seen on peeling back that sheet.

Throughout that evening I had been obsessed with the wounds I had seen, especially on his forehead, and with some idea that the pictures might not come out properly, or might not show the injuries adequately, I had stayed up hour after hour trying to sketch what I had seen. It had been compulsive. I had drawn sketch after sketch, running into dozens, all of which seemed inadequate.

But the sketches hadn't been necessary. The pictures had come out well, and many copies had been printed—which was fortunate, because the negatives were stolen shortly after from our *Daily Dispatch* photographic library, in spite of heavy security.

Often as a reporter I had been surprised at how readily bereaved people cooperated with the press. The news editor would send you to interview parents whose child had been killed in an accident and to ask for a picture of the child. I had always shrunk from this, expecting the parents to be outraged; yet every time they had been eager to oblige. I concluded it had something to do with the wish of bereaved people to share their loss as widely as possible—to state it to the world in their pain. To supply a picture of the dead child to a newspaper was somehow to mark the child's death more significantly, to state the child's identity as a being who had lived and been loved, to spread the grief.

I had similar feelings on watching this scene being filmed. While it was a painful evocation of the real event, it was a powerful recording— probably the most powerful possible recording in media terms—of how Steve Biko had been killed, and it would now be shared with countless millions who would see this film all over the world.

On one level all that was happening was that professional actors were performing in front of a camera to the dictates of a script and a director. But on another level this mundane process was becoming the means of literally telling the world what I wanted to be known as widely as possible—that Steve Biko had been beaten to death by ruthless functionaries whose murderous deeds had for too long been hidden from that world.

Steve Biko was the forty-fifth South African to die violently in South African Security Police custody. His killers, the killers of the other forty-four, had not been publicly exposed sufficiently; smooth-talking South African ambassadors abroad were still being invited to genteel lunches and seminars. But this scene, surely, would help to change that, would stoke the indignation of ordinary people from Kansas City to Kamchatka so that the emissaries of apartheid would never again have the same reception from the citizens of the world outside.

This was what made this reenactment important to me—that an event in a small mortuary in King William's Town in 1977 should surface widely in the world to haunt the people responsible. And that was why I felt a kind of exultation along with the rekindled grief at the accuracy of the mortuary scene.

In fact, the main purpose of this entire film for me was that it should result in a new awareness in the world of the real nature of apartheid—that apartheid had depths of horror that the world was not yet aware of and that more had to be done by governments everywhere to unite to rid the human race of this scourge.

Film had done the same to inform the world about Nazism. To give a recent example, millions had been horrified on seeing *Sophie's Choice* to learn that it was possible for a human being to force a mother to choose death for one of her children—yet many of the people horrified by Nazism were not well enough informed to put apartheid in the same bracket, and to realize that similar outrages were being perpetrated daily in the name of the same obscene creed of "racial purity." There were even some Jews who had suffered racial persecution in Nazi Germany, yet who now, as citizens of Israel, saw nothing wrong in Israeli military cooperation with the South African regime. They, and people all over the world, had to be made aware that *Herrenvolk* racism was alive and thriving in South Africa.

There was no more powerful medium in the world than a major feature film, not even television, and it was this thought that tempered my aversion to the mortuary scene.

Still, it was the worst to watch being made.

Denzel Washington had to lie for long periods in the "shelf," as still as a dead body; the only minor detail that was different from the actual event was that in the King William's Town mortuary there had been no cranking device to raise or lower the trolley for the bodies to be slid out on to.

The outside of the mortuary building had only one deficiency—there was no sign reading NON-WHITE SECTION—and this was soon put right. Bob Betts, one of the "cockney quintet," stenciled the sign, "aging" it with a mixture of coffee dregs and water.

There was also a fine performance in the mortuary scene from Kevin McNally, who played the part of Ken, a *Daily Dispatch* photographer who took pictures of Biko's body while the mortuary attendant was out of the room. The character of Ken was based partly on Gavin Robson, a reporter-photographer who had taken some of the Biko pictures and who later escaped from South Africa in the trunk of a car crossing the border into Botswana after considerable harassment by the Security Police following my own banning and escape. After escaping, Gavin

112

Robson worked in New York for a time before settling in Canada. The character "Ken" was also based partly on Fraser MacLean, an American photographer on the *Dispatch* who took many of the Biko pictures.

Kevin McNally had come out to play the composite part, which originally hadn't been a major one; but Attenborough was so impressed with his screen quality, as seen in the rushes, that between them they fashioned it into a stronger role.

The camera also "loved" Kevin McNally; at the daily rushes when he appeared there was always a reaction from those watching. It was often one of amusement, because he had a subtle comedic sense. He possessed the skill of the born screen actor: his underplaying and "thinking" on-screen positively bounced out onto the audience.

Off-camera he kept us highly amused, and seemed to have a running fight against Zimbabwean insect life and microbes, for which he had a special dread. There was allegedly this minuscule creature he had read about, encountered in certain waters, that entered every orifice in the human body and laid hundreds of eggs. Wherever it existed—perhaps only in the McNally mind—it didn't exist in Zimbabwe. But that didn't stop him worrying about it . . .

He was also apprehensive about spiders and diseases, at which Kevin Kline started listening hard, because the script called for him to enter the waters of the Zambezi River. Kline had heard about the horrors of the waterborne disease of bilharzia. A clean-living American boy from Saint Louis, Missouri, now living in New York, Kline was trooper enough to enter the Zambezi, but wanted certain tests done first. These were duly done with no problems resulting, because bilharzia was seldom encountered in moving waters and one thing the Zambezi did was *move*.

A more dangerous presence in the waters of the Zambezi was the crocodile. Attenborough had marksmen posted nearby to shoot any crocs that might menace Kevin as he waded in.

The other Kevin, McNally, had a strange encounter with an ant in Mutare while we were filming there. He was sitting on a step near the set when he saw a large Zimbabwean ant, almost a centimeter long, dozing in the sun. To see its reaction he prodded it with a lollipop stick, and the ant, enraged, seized the stick from him and, he swears, brandished it at him. He evacuated the area immediately, shaken.

I had reason to know that Zimbabwe ants were special. On one of my visits to "Rhodesia" I had seen an interesting use of ants—to prospect for gold. Scientists at an institute near Harare (née Salisbury) had found that anthills could yield traces of gold which had been brought up to the surface and excreted by the ants, and the position of these traces in the anthills indicated the position and depth at which the gold seam was to be found. Where you found an anthill with enough signs of gold, you just dug down for the stuff. The idea of using ants for gold prospecting had seemed absurd at first, but when the scientists at the institute had produced positive results, their findings had been taken seriously in other countries with similar deposits.

Kevin McNally also had a morbid interest in crocodiles.

Most of the members of the cast had never seen crocodiles, and few of them believed crocs could jump, and jump high. I hadn't known this when I had first seen the sight myself, at Lake Kariba in Zimbabwe. I had been about to photograph a large crocodile as it slept in the sun when it leapt suddenly up at a tree branch on which a bird had settled. It missed the bird, but its jaws snapped shut with an appalling sound. That massive creature had jumped fully seven feet into the air.

We had no crocodiles in South Africa, except in zoos or on the remote northern borders, though that fact hadn't stopped one American publication from reporting in 1978 that on my escape I had swum a "crocodile-infested" river. If the Telle River had had crocodiles I wouldn't have gone near it, let alone waded into it.

On the day after my escape into Lesotho it was widely reported that I had crossed the border by swimming, and while I had never made such a claim I was at least partly responsible for the misunderstanding which had given rise to the story. The people helping me to escape had asked me to create confusion about when and where I had crossed over, to "cover" them for as long as possible before the Security Police started asking questions around the neighborhood. When journalists came to interview me at the British High Commisson in Maseru I decided to try to lay a false trail without actually lying.

After I had declined to tell them exactly how I had made the crossing, the reporter from the *Johannesburg Sunday Express* said: "You must have swum the river," and I replied: "It's not a very wide river, you know." I went on to say that the Telle was normally a narrow stream, and that the flood conditions of the past six days had been unseasonal; but by now several had latched onto the direct question about swimming and my oblique answer to it, and they ran the story of me swimming across the flooded river.

I refused to confirm or deny this, as it was useful in drawing attention away from the border post through which I had actually gone. It was more than a week later in England that the direct question was put to me: "Did you swim that river?" I replied that I had not, but felt I couldn't say specifically how I had got across.

Two further weeks went by before the South African Security Police apparently gave up trying to pinpoint the place of the swim and considered the possibility that I might have been brazen enough to go through the border post. They finally checked with the border officials, who mentioned that on the day in question a priest had crossed through. Journalists following this up asked if it were true that I had crossed the border "disguised as an Anglican priest," and I replied that it was not. I didn't explain that I had been disguised as a *Catholic* priest. If they had simply said "priest" I would have had a problem.

After a further delay, during which I was reassured that the trail to my helpful friends was now cold, I told as much detail as I felt I could about the escape without incriminating them. Still, the swimming story persisted in a number of publications—one of which added the crocodile touch for good measure.

To film the Telle Bridge sequences the unit switched its operations to the valley of the Macheke River in a remote corner of Zimbabwe near the Mozambique border. The scenes to be shot here would cover my crossing over in disguise, then Wendy's crossing over with the children.

These sequences took a week, and we grew to know that deserted little part of Zimbabwe well. It took the convoy an hour and a half to reach the location every day, yet no matter how early we would get there the tents and caravans would be there and all departments functioning by the time of our arrival—including John Mollo with his *Times* crossword puzzle.

115

It was the classic case of the imperturbable Englishman. There we were only a few miles from Mozambique where a guerrilla war was being fought between the Frelimo government of Samora Machel and the Renamo rebels backed by South Africa, with every possibility that the South Africans might ask their client guerrillas to pay a passing call on this presumptuous band of people making a nasty antiapartheid film. We were sitting ducks for mortar fire, yet there was Mollo on his folding chair at his folding table, murmuring thoughtfully: "Strikebound in six letters . . . hmmm . . ."

Location manager Allan James was busy elsewhere the day I decided to find out about relocation logistics, so I sought out Rory Kilalea, the location manager (Zimbabwe), to learn how the unit managed to have the tents and caravans up so quickly and so far from their last site; how they always remained until we left late at night, yet relocated many miles away before we arrived early the next morning.

He explained that they had two sets, even of the big marquees we ate in, and that they were pitched in a leapfrogging operation so that they'd always be ready for early or late work by the unit—the new camp established before the old one was dismantled.

The morning I crossed the border was the most frightening of my life. After ducking the police searchlight the night before, I had found the river too flooded to wade or swim across with the bag I was carrying. The bag, a South African Airways presentation from my VIP days before the banning, contained the manuscript of my book on Steve Biko. This would have been political dynamite if found, not only because of its contents and because in writing it I had broken the restrictions forbidding me to write anything, but because the book ended with an appeal for international economic sanctions against South Africa—then considered a treasonous and capital offense.

Because I had to get to Maseru by ten A.M., my only chance now was to go through the border post with the fake Irish passport I was carrying as an identity cover.

Moments before the gate of the border post was opened, I had a fantastic bit of luck—a Lesotho postal inspector drove up in his Land Rover and offered me a lift across. As he was well-known to the officials

"Monarch of all he surveys..." Attenborough atop a high camera tower in the Macheke Valley near the Mozambique border, preparing to shoot the scene in which the Woods family escapes into Lesotho.

Donald and Wendy Woods *(above)*, Penelope Wilton and Kevin Kline *(opposite)*, on the beach near Mombasa, Kenya, for the scene in which Donald and Wendy Woods have an argument about leaving South Africa.

Attenborough on the set.

A light moment with
Lady Attenborough.

A tracking shot in Kenya, as Penelope Wilton and Kevin Kline prepare to reenact a scene.

Even the goats had to obey first assistant director
David Tomblin...

Attenborough does his foot-stomping version of the Xhosa dance Donald Woods did after getting across the border; Kevin Kline prepares to reenact the dance.

Kevin Kline with John Hargreaves, who plays the part of Bruce, the Australian friend who helped Donald Woods get to Maseru during his escape from South Africa.

Kevin Kline about to cross
through the border post
with the *Biko* manuscript.

on both sides of the bridge, and as they assumed I was traveling with him and known to him, they barely glanced at my "passport."

Kevin Kline and Joe Marcell, who played the postal inspector, went through an exchange of dialogue virtually identical to the one I'd had with the real inspector, even to his saying his name was Moses. Some members of the unit assumed the part about his name being Moses had been a Briley invention to add a touch of humor, and I enjoyed telling them it was true.

After I had reached London some journalists had tracked Moses down in Lesotho and had interviewed him about the incident. He had been surprised that the "nice priest" had been a political outlaw. As Saint Theresa's mission was only a few miles from the border, and as priests from there had often crossed over to say Mass in Qthing in Lesotho, the priest disguise had been ideal.

Briley and Attenborough had included in the script another incident which had really occurred that morning. After Moses and I had crossed through both checkpoints on either side of the bridge, and before Moses returned to take the wheel on the Lesotho side, I was standing alone looking back at South African territory and realizing fully that I had actually got out. In exultation I broke into a *xensa*—a Xhosa dance in which the feet are stamped and the body is shaken energetically— then had looked up to see the bemused Lesotho officials staring at this odd sight of a white priest doing the *xensa*.

Kevin Kline had watched me trying with some embarrassment to reenact this dance for him to emulate, and I hadn't found it easy. Usually inhibited when it came to dancing, I had found it easy on the morning of my escape when it had happened spontaneously, but to do it now "in cold blood" in front of the whole unit was something of a trial. But again the Kline talents were equal to the challenge, and he did it so well that you would have thought the *xensa* was as endemic to Missouri as to the Transkei Territory.

Stuart Craig had again excelled with the set. The border post was so like the original one at Telle Bridge, even to the look of the sheds on both sides and the wired-in compounds—though his bridge was longer than the real one—that it was odd to think these buildings would be dismantled when we left.

117

The many shots involving Kevin Kline, Joe Marcell, the border officials, and the various perspectives of the bridge took two days to shoot, and in the heat of the valley as summer was coming on a sudden outbreak of elastic-band warfare broke out among members of the unit. It was started by Frank Connor, the stills photographer, who aimed a stretched elastic band at Nikki Clapp and got her right between the shoulder blades. She tried to retaliate, but missed Frank and hit Jason Lehel, and the war escalated from there. Where all the elastic bands sprouted from in that remote spot I can't imagine, but it was like a proliferation of the arms race, and soon the air was thick with these stinging little missiles.

David Tomblin noticed this going on and lumbered over to join in, but the expert who emerged with the deadliest aim was Eddie Collins, the cameraman. When Attenborough was around there was a tacit truce, but the minute his back was turned the barrage recommenced. It finally spent itself when all available ammunition was expended.

Frank Connor, half Irish and half Italian, always looked as if he had just been woken up and hadn't had time to grab enough clothes. Wearing only the barest necessities, he appeared to be dressed mainly in a large assortment of cameras ready to fire from the hip. The results of all this apparent disorganization were very good indeed, and apart from his fine pictures and those of his colleagues Simon Mein and Jody Boulting now gracing this book, his selections of stills of scenes from the film were the first visual indication we had that we were involved in a film of unusual quality. Diana Hawkins had designed an album of pictures suggested and chosen by her to give a preliminary impression of the key sequences of the film, and this had captured the power of the film strikingly through his pictures in black and white.

Frank felt at times that some members of the crew didn't realize why he had to get as close to the action as he did, but he never let this inhibit him, and often reminded me of a press photographer in his determination to get into the right position for the shot. More than once he roughly elbowed one of the technical advisers (me) out of the way, and when I saw the photographic result I was glad he had.

It was at about this time that Norman Spencer thought up what would later become the title of our film.

At first, because the film was based on my two books *Biko* and *Asking for Trouble*, the provisional working title for the project, until a proper title could be agreed, was *Biko/Asking for Trouble*. For months we all tried to think up a good title, and the first one that most of us were enthusiastic about was *State of Emergency*. That, we thought, was that. Then it was discovered that this title had been registered by a film company for a project already under production, so we had to start all over again.

Literally hundreds of titles were listed for consideration, none of which seemed to click as obviously perfect. The one the people at Universal liked best among these—and that preliminary research persuaded them would suit the film best—was one scribbled down by Norman in between takes one morning.

It was *Cry Freedom*.

None of us liked it much, not even Norman, but we were all casting about so desperately by now that almost any vaguely appropriate combination of words was being added to the list for consideration. So it was sent along to Universal to be added to the list. When it was finally decided upon in April 1987, many of us still had reservations about it. Wasn't it too pompous? Too pretentious? Couldn't we find something less direct; less "on the nose"?

No, we couldn't.

Then, as titles often tend to do once they are firmly decided on, it began to sound not so bad. Even increasingly right. Norman liked to tell of how hard the air ministry in Britain had found it to agree on a name for a remarkable new fighter plane which was later to change the course of history. There had been initial derision when someone senior in the air ministry had settled the issue by reaching for his volume of Shakespeare and turning to *Macbeth*. His edict was: The name shall be Spitfire.

"Spitfire?" hollered everyone. "What a crazy name for a plane!"

Norman also told of how a similar edict from movie mogul Darryl F. Zanuck had ended attempts to call a certain film *Flying Crazy*. No, said Zanuck. Call it *Those Magnificent Men in Their Flying Machines*. Members of the unit had clutched their heads in anguish. What a crazy name for a movie!

And now here we were with *Cry Freedom*.

It wasn't subtle. It wasn't complex. None of us liked it. But it began to take hold . . .

Now came the turn of Penelope Wilton and the children to reenact the scene of Wendy and our children crossing the same border that evening as "tourists," and here the rain machine was brought into operation.

Not having seen movie rain being used before, and not always having found movie rain convincing, I was impressed with this machine and with its effects on the screen. Of German design, it consisted of a high tower with a strong jet of water which fragmented and fell as rainwater does, by gravity, and it was augmented by two spray machines which combined to give a proper appearance of a real Southern African downpour. More than 100,000 gallons of water were pumped from the river and chemically treated against bilharzia and other germs before falling as "rain." The overall effect was so convincing that even the frogs were fooled into croaking.

What was strange was the demarcation line between the rained-on area and the rest of the place, which hadn't had rain for many weeks. In one spot you stood in dry late-winter Zimbabwe; two yards away in a summer downpour, with all the rain-engaged members of the unit walking around in yellow oilskins and Wellington boots.

In the wet darkness, except for the strategically placed lights of Ronnie Taylor, it was a scene of misery as "Wendy" and the children took leave of her parents and headed across the bridge. There being virtually no dialogue in this part of the sequence, except for the grandparents' good-byes to the children, I had sneaked off to Kevin Kline's caravan at the tent camp a half mile away and fallen into a deep sleep. Attenborough had then seen through the back of his head that I wasn't where I should have been and had sent a radio message to locate me.

I was roused from sleep and summoned to the monsoon area, donning gum boots and a rain slicker to approach Attenborough through the torrents.

He greeted me with his customary affection, then looking into my bleary eyes he said with a straight face: "Donald, darling, I just wanted to know what Jane's grandfather would call her in saying good-bye—would he have a pet name for her?"

I told him he would call her Jane. And as I sloshed back through the mud I called him a number of names, none of which was "Dickie darling."

I felt sorry for the actors, especially the children, who had to keep getting drenched in the downpour time after time. After each scene they would be dried off and kept warm with heaters in their tents, then recostumed and brought back for another drenching. The worst part was when, having been escorted to their positions by members of the wardrobe and props department who held umbrellas over their heads to protect them from the rain until the last possible moment, they would suddenly be abandoned by order of David Tomblin as the full force of the water hit them. Relentlessly thorough, Attenborough ordered several takes of each scene in the rain, of which there were about seven, involving a different camera setup each time. The cameras were protected from the rain by waterproof plastic.

The children put up stoically with all this drenching, and though it was kept to the minimum necessary, that night was the worst of all the filming for them, as for the hairdressers and wardrobe people. But months later, while in London for dubbing dialogue, the kids said it had been their most enjoyable scene!

I stopped counting the number of times Tomblin uttered the strange words: "Kill the rain!"

Shortly before dawn on the final morning, after we had filmed through the night and were waiting to shoot a scene at around sunrise, Steve Chigorimbo, overcome at the beauty of the rose-tinted sky above the surrounding mountains, burst out with: "Oh, but Africa is beautiful!" Then, feeling this might have been seen as an excess of continental pride, he added bashfully: ". . . Even if I say it myself."

It occurred to me that morning that one of the most vital departments in the unit was the electrical department, because no matter where we needed power, and regardless of some of the outlandish spots we filmed at, theirs was the notable achievement of bringing along the generators and connecting them all up to supply as much power as if we were filming in the heart of London.

No one could tell me where the term *gaffer* came from—not even gaffer Alan Martin—nor why Dave Moore's job as his assistant was described as "best boy." Their lights also had catchy names. The small ones were called "babies," the medium ones "bashers," and the big ones "brutes." Then there were the super-big ones—the "dinos." They had their own in-group language too in the electrical department, wherein a bulb was called a "bubble"; there were no doubt other terms as well, the code for which was not broken by the rest of us.

With the filming in the eastern highlands now completed, we all made ready to leave for Harare for the last stretch of filming there before the sequences in Kenya and, back in England, at Shepperton Studios. Our cars were ready in the Macheke Valley, and as Attenborough nodded to Tomblin for the last time to call "Kill the rain!" Norman and I swiftly climbed into our car, to be driven to Harare. I looked back at the electricians, conscious they would still be there for hours after we were asleep.

Much as the members of the unit had enjoyed the rural scenery, particularly around the attractive town of Mutare nestled among the hills of the Zimbabwe border, there was general anticipation of the return to Harare.

Many of us had grown fond of the city—the golfing fraternity because of the wide variety of courses, and the eaters because of the broader range of restaurants in the capital. After two months, hotel food had become a trial.

Some members of the crew were enthusiastic Harare-boosters on account of the climate, the bougainvillea, the jacarandas, and the clean look of the city.

We returned to Harare in time to meet Wendy at the airport and prepare for some of the most dramatic scenes in the film, beginning with the reenactment of the interrogation of Steve Biko at the Security Police office in King William's Town in 1976.

In this incident the interrogating officer (played in the film by Timothy West) had tried to show his power over Biko by striking out at him, but Biko had caught his fist. The officer had then appeared to relent, but as two other Security Police officers held Biko down in a chair he had hit Biko across the face. Biko had then lunged out of the chair and hit him back. What had stopped all three of them assaulting Biko was the fact that he had to give evidence in a trial in Pretoria and they hadn't wanted marks of assault on him.

Watching Timothy West in this scene, Wendy and I noticed again how well the top actors *moved*, how much talent there was in simply looking and acting natural before the camera, and how this was done through convincing use of the *unobvious* gestures people normally make.

In a suit and broad tie of that time, and with a small mustache, Timothy West reminded me strongly of the officer he was portraying. This man, whose real name was Gerhardus Hattingh, had had the nickname "Seksie" among his colleagues in the Security Police. Short for *seksie leier* (section leader) it sounded incongruously like "sexy." A thickset man in his fifties, "Seksie" Hattingh had been notorious in the Eastern province for his hounding of the Biko group.

Afrikaners generally love nicknames, and these are seldom subtle. Foreign Minister Roelof Botha is called "Pik" ("Peewee" or "Tiny") because he is a big man, and sports heroes have nicknames like "Platvoet" ("Flatfoot") Pretorius and "Windhond" ("Greyhound") Muller. In the Security Police some of the nicknames are more ominous, like that of "Spyker" ("Nail") Van Wyk of Cape Town, whose torture specialty during interrogation is said to be the hammering of a nail through the foreskin of the prisoner.

Much though people in the rest of the world disapprove of apartheid, there is still massive ignorance abroad of the extent of sadism and viciousness inflicted on black dissidents in the interrogation cells of the Security Police in South Africa. There is also gratuitous viciousness against black institutions which don't toe the government line, and against the property of these institutions, as we were able to show by reenacting another authentic event.

The scene I most enjoyed watching being filmed was the next major scene we shot, not because of any special skills or techniques employed but because it had for me a special significance. This was the reenactment of the Security Police raid by night on the Black Community Centre established by Biko's group in Leopold Street. Wearing balaclava masks to hide their faces, the Security Police officers had smashed everything of value or use they could find in that center, in the most wanton exercise of pointless destruction I had ever witnessed. I relished the idea that that act of malicious destruction by the King William's Town Security Police—an act they had obviously regarded as just another job—would one day be witnessed by many millions of moviegoers all over the world in a damning reenactment.

Most white South Africans claim that apartheid is motivated by fear of the black majority, and the South African government addresses all its propaganda to the world on the basis that the white minority fears being "swamped" by the black majority. But the savage wrecking of a self-help project run by young blacks in King William's Town in 1976—the smashing of typewriters, slashing of furniture, breaking of equipment, burning of a car—this deed had nothing to do with fear. This was a deed of hate. And this, ultimately, was what *Cry Freedom* was about—to tell the world of the true nature of apartheid; that it was essentially a creed of hate and revulsion against persons of another skin color.

The set was another Stuart Craig masterpiece. He had seen the original former church in Leopold Street, King William's Town, and had re-created its atmosphere and appearance here in Harare. The set-dresser, Michael Seirton, another *Gandhi* Academy Award-winner on Attenborough's team, had provided an authentic look to the inside and to the booths for various activities such as dressmaking, pottery, typing instruction, and carpentry.

I remembered the depth of anger I had felt on looking at the scene of destruction the morning after the real raid. Black South Africans had so little to begin with anyway, yet even this small-scale attempt by blacks to develop practical skills had been regarded as intolerable by persons claiming allegiance to what they described as "Christian Western values." Outside the wrecked center had been an old car used for the teaching of basic mechanical knowledge; this had been burned by the Security Police. But what had angered me most had been the sight of smashed typewriters and the slashing of the few old chairs and settees.

It was my reporting of this vandalism that had led to my being sentenced to six months in prison, as would be reflected in the ensuing film sequences.

I had gone to Pretoria and told Police Minister Kruger, hoping he would take action against his Security Police or at least send them a strong signal to stop this kind of thing. I had also mentioned the raid to the head of the dreaded Bureau of State Security, General Hendrik

Van den Bergh, a very tall gray-haired man with rimless spectacles.

Knowing these people was sometimes a strange experience. Once at the Holiday Inn in Johannesburg General Van den Bergh had said to me out of the blue while sipping vodka and tomato juice: "You and I have only one thing in common, Mr. Woods—we both regard P. W. Botha as a rubbish!" It had astonished me that he should say this of a cabinet colleague to a member of the "enemy"—the English-language press. Clearly his deep dislike of Botha, who was later to edge him and Vorster out of office, had got the better of his discretion. Or perhaps at the time he had regarded me as less of an enemy, because I was South Africa's delegate to the International Chess Federation for a forthcoming congress in Switzerland at which the Russians would move for the expulsion of our federation from the world body.

It was ironical, as I was out on bail pending appeal against the prison sentence imposed in consequence of my visit to Kruger.

The next big scene to be shot was the reenactment of the incident in which I went to see Police Minister Kruger and told him of the smashing up of the Black Community Centre by his Security Police. I had seen the minister at his house on a Saturday, and the house Stuart Craig found to represent the Kruger house was magnificent.

This was the fifth approach by a film company to use the house as a set, and the previous four requests had been turned down. Our request had been granted because of the theme of *Cry Freedom*. The owner of the house turned out to be Mrs. Jackie Narracott, formerly of Cape Town, who had attended a student protest meeting I had addressed there in September 1977 after Steve Biko's death, and who had been among the first of many to write us supportive letters when we had escaped from South Africa. Here we now were, about to record on film some of the events of that time, in her house half a continent away from Cape Town.

Visiting us to watch some of the filming on location was a family friend, Jann Turner, and when she and Jackie Narracott were introduced they exchanged incredulous greetings; they had been family friends in Cape Town fourteen years earlier.

Jann's father, Dr. Richard Turner, had been a university lecturer in Grahamstown, near East London, and later in Durban, and had been a close friend of Steve Biko. He had been banned and restricted to his home in Durban, and when he heard of our escape he had exultantly phoned his wife Barbara, who was away in Cape Town. Shortly after this there was a knock at the door, and when he went to see who was there he was shot at point-blank range. He died in the presence of his two little daughters, Kim, aged seven, and Jann, aged ten.

Officially nobody was suspected of the killing, but it occurred during a spate of attacks on banned people by members of the security police and their friends acting as "off-duty" vigilantes. There had been a shotgun blast through the front door of Dr. Fatima Meer, another banned person, and there had been other similar incidents such as the T-shirt attack on our child Mary, as well as the earlier shooting at our house previously.

When the smooth-talking ambassadors and consuls of South Africa present to the television screens of the world their expressions of wounded innocence, they are too seldom challenged about the murderous activities of their Security Police. The awful thing about people like Kruger and Vorster is that they gave every public indication of admiration and support of Security Police methods, even when they were privately expressing their condemnation of "excesses."

I had gone to see Kruger in his ministerial house in Pretoria, and the Narracott house was a good representation of the Kruger lifestyle. The house was set on a hilltop in the countryside north of Harare, and was part of an estate measuring hundreds of acres. Sweeping lawns went up in terraces to the façade, which had two wings and an overall style of Cape Dutch modern. Bougainvillea and bright flowerbeds flanked the lawns, and there was a view down across some low-lying hills of the valley and a lake in the distance.

John Thaw played the part of Kruger—an inspired piece of casting by Attenborough, who before casting anyone else in the entire production was certain that Thaw would make a perfect Kruger. He did. Those who knew him from the screen as an abrasive cop were in for a surprise at his convincing portrayal of the plausible politician oozing charm and reassurance. We told him that for years his flying-squad program *The Sweeney* had been on South African television, dubbed into Afrikaans as *Blitspatrollie* (*Lightning Patrol*), and he said he had known this, because he had received fan letters in Afrikaans.

We doubted that he'd get any in that language for his Kruger portrayal in *Cry Freedom*.

After the Kruger scene we moved to the Charles Prince Airport, a small civil-aviation and flying-club airfield on the outskirts of Harare, to do the scenes reenacting the day the British deputy high commissioner to Lesotho, Jim Moffatt, and his wife, Pam, had seen us off on our flight from Maseru to Botswana, after threats that South African planes would force us down.

Members of the unit who thought the Charles Prince Airport had something to do with the heir to the British throne learned that it was in fact named after a past doyen of the local flying club, Mr. Charlie Prince, inevitably nicknamed "Bonnie" by his friends. Here we had two Australian actors, John Hargreaves and Nicholas Tate—the latter playing the part of the New Zealander, Richie de Montauk, who had piloted the plane.

Jim Moffatt, played by Alec McCowen, and his wife had been parental in their care and hospitality. A smiling man with a fine sense of humor, Jim had had us laughing with his cowboy monologues, one of which always began: "*Who* will carry the mail through Dead Man's Gulch?"

Alec McCowen also had a good sense of humor, and a habit, which amused Nick Tate, of repeating quietly to himself from time to time, à propos of nothing, isolated phrases from Cole Porter songs . . .

"Hm. Yes. Well. Now, heaven knows, anything goes."

The Britten-Norman Islander at this airfield was a real one. Later there'd be a fake one, or part of one, at Shepperton for some interior shots of the family. I enjoyed climbing into the reliable little plane again and reliving those tense hours in the air over South African territory, this time in complete safety.

On the day of the actual flight I had kept looking at my watch disbelievingly, because the minute hand had seemed to crawl along with agonizing slowness. The flight across South African territory had lasted two hours and twenty minutes, and I had kept staring out of the plane's window to see if the South African government's threat was to be carried out. Then I'd look around the little cabin, seeing the members of my family, and wondering: "What have I got them into?" I'd reassure myself that Pretoria had been bluffing . . . then I'd think: "What if they aren't? They've done crazy things before. Are the lives of these children in danger?"

Wendy had seemed unconcerned, with Mary asleep in her arms. Gavin and Duncan had treated it as an interesting excursion, scuffling from time to time in their seats. Dillon and Jane had known the score, and Dillon, who had a precise mind on such matters, had kept track of our progress across the map.

I'd resisted looking at my watch for what I was sure had been fifteen minutes—then looked to find only four minutes had elapsed.

Now, on the set, sitting in the little plane, I was reliving it all as I looked at the familiar instrument panel and structure of the windows— grateful that all had worked out as I hadn't known it would on that day.

Cry Freedom was helping me to exorcise a lot of buried trauma and forgotten angst.

The final scene we shot in Harare was on a set constructed near our hotel. It was the sequence of Steve Biko taking me to a shebeen, or illegal drinking den in the township, then to have supper with a township family. At one stage there had been a suggestion that the shebeen scene might better be shot back at Shepperton, and I had heard Attenborough asking Terry Clegg: "Has the shebeen moved to England?"

In the shebeen scene Attenborough and Eddie Collins decided to try an ambitious 180-degree shot which required complicated snatching away of walls and chairs with precise timing so that the camera could sweep around. The scene took about nine hours as Terry Clegg wandered around muttering irritably to himself about what he described as cinematic masturbation.

In the course of this operation Attenborough also got the mutters. But in the end they got the scene shot, and it looked very good in the rushes.

Initially Attenborough, disappointed at the lack of zest in the Zimbabwean extras doing the dancing in the shebeen and unable to get them to keep time to the jazzy music, came out of the smoky atmosphere murmuring with a wicked smile at the inversion of the cliché: "They have an *amazing* lack of rhythm . . ."

But the dancing came right, particularly when Wendy noticed, outside, a standby named Cephas uninhibitedly doing the dance the others inside hadn't been able to get right. She told Attenborough, Attenborough recruited Cephas and several other members of the crew who could do the dance well, and the scene proceeded with the requisite rhythm and verve.

While we were doing the scene in the township house, Denzel Washington discovered during the course of an off-camera conversation with a Zimbabwean woman playing one of the parts in the scene, that she had been Steve Biko's teacher in high school for several years. The woman, Nocebo Mlambo, was originally from King William's Town, and we clustered around her for anecdotes about the schoolboy Biko she had known.

She said he had been an obvious leader even at the age of fifteen, and was always at the forefront of a class petition. He had been exceptionally bright in class, and popular with the other pupils, although he had never seemed to be trying to dominate them. What she remembered most about him from that time, and what had stuck most in her mind to make him different from the others, was what she recalled as a highly developed sense of fairness, an unusually deep attachment, for one of that age, to the *idea* of justice.

The last shot in Zimbabwe completed, we returned to the hotel to pack for the charter flight to Kenya, glad we had finished on schedule and that we had had ninety days of rainless weather to shoot in.

The next day it poured with rain! The Zimbabwean skies had considerately waited three months for us to finish before unleashing a typical Southern African deluge in which the great drops pounded down.

That night hundreds of Zimbabwean guests were invited for the grand "wrap party," and a good time was had by all—notably by our young medic, Keith Stack, who celebrated having brought us all through the schedule undiseased and unharmed. When I phoned him to say goodbye the next morning he said he was feeling somewhat fragile.

My prevailing thought as we left Zimbabwe was that the country and its people had been exceptionally kind to us and supportive of our project, and that we had been very fortunate to have completed the schedule without once being attacked or hampered by the South African government's "dirty tricks squad." Whether this was due to the effectiveness of our security arrangement, or whether Pretoria had decided an attack on the project might be counterproductive, nobody could know. There was, however, a third possibility—that their hands were so full in trying to put down the internal unrest within South Africa that they had bigger fish to fry.

During our stay in Zimbabwe we had arranged for South African newspapers to be sent to us regularly and had telephoned friends in various parts of South Africa. We found that the degree of misinformation about Zimbabwe among South Africans was prodigious. They had an image of a country wracked with racial hatreds and tensions, on the point of massive intertribal war, governed by a Marxist dictator and practically run direct from the Kremlin in Moscow. We tried, in most cases in vain, to disabuse them of this ludicrous caricature of Zimbabwean reality. Most were simply too brainwashed to respond.

The flight from Harare to Mombasa was uneventful, though it was good to catch a glimpse of Lake Malawi and of the country I believe to be the most beautiful in the world. Take Scotland with all its variety and put it down in Central Africa, and you have Malawi.

I have twice visited Malawi. After the first visit I thought I must have exaggerated its attractions to myself, but after going there a second time in 1973 I realized it was even better than I had remembered.

First drawn to it after reading Laurens Van der Post's book *Venture to the Interior*, I went with two colleagues from the *Daily Dispatch* to witness its independence celebrations in 1964. We were quartered in the press hostel in Blantyre, and on the first morning were driving to a press conference when we saw the two correspondents from *Pravda* and *Izvestia* walking. Never having met Russians, we gave them a lift, and one of them was fluent in English.

To make conversation I said: "If our government knew we were giving a lift to two Russians we'd be imprisoned."

The English-speaking one replied instantly: "If *ourr* government knew we were *yaccepting*—we'd be *yexecuted*!"

Malawi is so green, the mountains so big, the huge lake so deep and blue, and there is such a profusion of mosses and giant ferns, that each turn of the road is like a picture.

In 1973 I realized a long-held ambition and took a week-long cruise on the lake. Lake Malawi is over four hundred miles long and about fifty miles wide at its widest. The cruise ship *Ilala* is one of four that take passengers and call in at the lakeside ports, and the palm-fringed bays and inlets and the shining white sand beaches make this look like a tropical ocean rather than a lake in the interior of a great continent. In the middle of the lake is Likoma Island, on which stands a great cathedral of the dimensions of Winchester Cathedral—built by the natives on their conversion to Christianity according to plans got for them by missionaries whom they told of their wish to build a church as great as one of the greatest in Europe. I walked among the cloisters there, crowned with tumbling bougainvillea, and marveled at these great dimensions in this isolated spot.

A curious fact about Lake Malawi is that the first naval engagement of the First World War took place on it. Malawi, then called Nyasaland, was one of Britain's colonies in 1914, while Tanzania, then called Tanganyika, was a German colony. The boundary between British and German territory was a line down the middle of Lake Nyasa, as it was called, and Britain had several ships and gunboats on the lake. So did the Germans, who controlled the eastern shore, with Cuxhaven as their main port.

The head of the British naval forces on the lake, Commander Rhoades, was friendly with his German counterpart, Kapitan Berndt, and they used to meet occasionally in midlake for drinks. When the war broke out Rhoades was ordered by telegraph to "clear the lake of German shipping," and set forth in HMS *Guendolen* after initial setbacks concerning armaments. The *Guendolen*'s only gun was an ancient two-pounder, and the only person to be found who could fire it was a character named "Champagne Charlie," who wore a monocle and frequented the bars of the British port, Fort Johnston.

Having recruited him, Rhoades eased the *Guendolen* quietly toward Cuxhaven where Berndt's ship, the *Wissman*, was drawn up on the slipway being repainted. The telegraph wires between Dar es Salaam and Cuxhaven had broken down, so Berndt had no way of knowing there was a war on, and was asleep in his quarters when the *Guendolen* started shelling the *Wissman*, scoring one hit amidships.

Kapitan Berndt, thinking Rhoades was drunk, flew into a rage and rowed out to the *Guendolen* in a dinghy shouting and swearing—to be helped on board, given a drink, and told he was a prisoner of war. The *Wissman* was towed back to Fort Johnston, repainted, and renamed HMS *King George V*.

On a visit to Fort Johnston I had seen in the local museum some relics of the famous engagement, which had been reported in *The Times*, though when first reports of it came through it was said that the men at the Admiralty had sent for maps to see precisely where this lake was. Perhaps they were surprised to discover that the lake they had never heard of was about the size of England . . .

One of the loveliest places in Malawi is the former capital, Zomba, where green-roofed houses are built on the hills; high above the town I stayed at a hotel whose rooms looked precipitously down from so high that the clouds appeared near enough to touch. The hotel bedrooms each had a wide picture window to display this view, and staying there was rather like having a large scenic cabin in an aircraft.

These thoughts all came back to me as we flew over Malawi on our way to the Kenyan resort of Mombasa.

When we landed it was unpleasantly humid, Mombasa being coastal and low-lying, not high up like Malawi and Zimbabwe. The drive to Diani Beach was a relief from the damp heat.

The next morning we drove mile after mile through palm groves stretching hundreds of yards back from the road. It was like Florida, in particular Key West, on a grander scale. The isolated beach we were to film at was not easy to reach, and our car bumped and ground its way along a rough-hewn road hastily fashioned by (who else?) Stuart Craig. I wondered how the huge trucks of the unit would get there, but—I might have known—they were there already.

Getting there was worth it. It was a pretty little beach and the vegetation was much like the vegetation back home on the wild coast of Transkei, South Africa. The only disappointment was that the waves were small.

Here we would shoot the scene of the argument between Wendy and me about leaving South Africa. She had objected to my announcing this without consulting her or discussing the matter. During shooting,

Penelope and Kevin gave it all they had, so that I started getting annoyed with Wendy all over again. Actually the argument raged over two beaches, for the sake of the camera angles, and this necessitated trekking over and through wild bush, where, amazingly, not a single snake showed itself.

This beach scene took a day and a half to film, as scheduled, and it completed our shooting in Africa.

It was a pity to leave Diani Beach without really getting to know it, but there was still a month of filming to complete at Shepperton Studios, so off we set for Mombasa airport en route for Nairobi and London.

At Mombasa airport we were well in time and stepped up to the check-in counter with foolish expectation. The first thing that should have warned us that all was not well was the complete absence of any human beings on the other side of the check-in counters. But the British are a stoic people, and everyone simply chose a seat to await the onset of routine service. When after a long time there was no sign of life on the official side of the counters, Terry Clegg went to investigate, and was told with quiet good humor by an official he managed to find that there was, actually, no plane.

No plane? But the unit was booked on two flights, each with flight numbers, confirmed by Kenya Airways the day before, for Nairobi.

Well, said the official, there *was* a flight, actually, but only one, not two, and the one was fully booked.

Clegg pointed out that this would have meant a massive overbooking when our flights were confirmed, an observation with which the official agreed wholeheartedly.

Somehow Clegg wangled about a dozen seats on the "fully booked" flight, then browbeat and bullied someone in Kenya Airways into providing a Fokker Friendship to take the rest of the unit to Nairobi. At one stage we noticed that he was now on the other side of the counter, not only checking in passengers on the flight himself but directing the Kenya Airways clerks in the checking in of others. It was impressive organization and initiative, and both sets of passengers reached Nairobi in time for the London flight.

Aboard the Fokker en route to Nairobi I thought of the story of the BBC radio commentator said to have interviewed a Spitfire pilot on the anniversary of the Battle of Britain. The pilot, Captain Van der Griendt of the Netherlands, said: "Ja, on dat day I vos trying to climb when zis fokker dived down on me . . ."

The BBC commentator broke in: "Er, if I may just point out to listeners, the Fokker is, of course, a make of German aircraft."

"No, no!" said Captain Van der Griendt. "Zis fokker vos a Messerschmitt!"

I hoped the story was true. If it wasn't I felt it ought to have been.

8

FINAL TOUCHES

London's Shepperton Studios seemed a confusing place: a strange mixture of the substantial and the transient. The hub of it was a solid old family mansion house with a glazed conservatory containing a statue of Alfred Hitchcock.

We used three of the big soundstages at Shepperton. One contained a township street to match an earlier sequence in Zimbabwe, another contained "our" house "inside out" for interior scenes, and a third contained a replica of what had been Steve Biko's office in Leopold Street, King William's Town.

These were stunning sets, particularly the first one, which contained the "township." This, I thought, was Stuart Craig at his brilliant best. What you saw, or seemed to see, was a street of houses. That is, you had an impression of more than twenty houses stretching into the distance and up onto a dark hillside, and the "street" of authentic-looking red Zimbabwe soil, pebbles and stones, appeared to be well over a hundred yards in extent. When I paced it out, however, I was amazed to find the whole perspective was only forty-nine paces long. Closer inspection also revealed that only the first house on the left was real and could be walked into and filmed in. The others, the further you got, were smaller and smaller, until the last three-dimensional one was barely chest high. Thereafter the houses were either two-dimensional silhouettes or paintings on the backdrop. But on the rushes the scene looked real, complete with a "real" tree with its branches moving in the breeze.

This set was used for a scene reenacting an incident in which the Security Police had knocked on Biko's door late at night in search of documents. He had stalled them at the door while Ntsiki hid the documents; he had managed to talk the officer into holding the search warrant up to a fairly high window, indicating when the exasperated officer should turn the page.

The real incident had been more dramatic than the version to be filmed: when the Security Police had finally gained access to the house one of them had had a pistol in his hand and Biko actually took it from him, saying: "No guns allowed in this house!" Amazingly the officer had let him get away with this; his gun had been handed back to him when the time came to leave. This was an extraordinary thing for a black man to get away with, but those who knew Steve Biko would have understood. His power of personality was unusual, and even the Security Police fell under its spell on occasion.

But Jack Briley left out the gun incident, feeling it would confuse audiences about the realities of the power balance between white Security Police and black dissidents. For the same reason he had at one time wanted to leave out the scene in which Biko had been hit across the face by a Security Police officer and had hit him back, but Attenborough had insisted on the scene, because the reason for the lack of Security Police retribution on this occasion could be given a plausible explanation: they hadn't wanted him to appear in court with marks of assault.

Biko had set out his own philosophy about resisting assault, and it might have supplied one of the clues as to how he came to be fatally assaulted. Shortly before his final arrest he said in an interview, when questioned about the possibility of being killed: "You are either alive and proud or you are dead, and when you are dead, you can't care anyway. And your method of death can itself be a politicizing thing. So you die in the riots. For a hell of a lot of them, in fact, there's really nothing to lose—almost literally, given the kind of situations that they come from. So if you can overcome the personal fear of death, which is a highly irrational thing, you know, then you're on the way. And in interrogation the same sort of thing applies. I was talking to this policeman, and I told him, 'If you want us to make any progress, the best thing is for us to talk. Don't try any form of rough stuff, because it just won't work.' And this is absolutely true also. For I could see what they could do to me which would make me all of a sudden soften to them. If they talk to me, well I'm bound to be affected by them as human beings. But the moment they adopt rough stuff, they are imprinting in my mind that they are police. And I only understand one form of dealing with police, and that's to be as unhelpful as possible. So I button up. And I told them this: 'It's up to you.' We had a boxing match the first day I was arrested. Some guy tried to clout me with a club. I went into him like a bull. I think he was under instructions to take it so far and no further, and using open hands so that he doesn't leave any marks on the face. And of course he said exactly what you were saying just now: 'I will kill you.' He meant to intimidate. And my answer was: 'How long is it going to take you?' Now of course they were observing my reaction. And they could see that I was completely unbothered. If they beat me up, it's to my advantage. I can use it. They just killed somebody in jail—a friend of mine—about ten days before I was arrested. Now it would have been bloody useful evidence for them to assault me. At least it would indicate what kind of possibilities were there, leading to this guy's death. So, I wanted them to go ahead and do what they could do, so that I could use it. I wasn't really afraid that their violence might lead me to make revelations I didn't want to make, because I had nothing to reveal on this particular issue. I was operating from a very good position, and they were in a very weak position. My attitude is, I'm not going to allow them to carry out their program faithfully. If they want to beat me five times, they can only do so on condition that I allow them to beat me five times. If I react sharply, equally and oppositely, to the first clap, they are not going to be able to systematically count the next four claps, you see. It's a fight. So if they had meant to give me so much of a beating, and not more, my idea is to make them go beyond what they wanted to give me and to give back as much as I can give so that it becomes an uncontrollable thing. You see the one problem this guy had with me: he couldn't really fight with me because it meant he must hit back, like a man. But he was given instructions, you see, on how to hit, and now these instructions were no longer applying because it was a fight. So he had to withdraw and get more instructions. So I said to them, 'Listen, if you guys want to do this your way, you have got to handcuff me and bind my feet together, so that I can't respond. If you allow me to respond, I'm certainly going to respond. And I'm afraid you may have to kill me in the process even if it's not your intention.' "

I had often speculated about the possibility that his death had resulted from his refusal to be cowed; his determination to talk back, give insult for insult and blow for blow. That he was outnumbered and captive in his final confrontation wouldn't necessarily have changed his attitude, and the Security Police would not necessarily have had the sense to perceive the logical result of their assault on someone who refused to be intimidated.

Filming in the studio with its controlled conditions and "silenceability" seemed to me so much easier than conveying all the heavy equipment around on location that I remarked to Norman that if I were a director I'd go for studio shooting every time. "Ah, you miss a lot by not going on location, depending on the type of film," said Norman. Of course we could not have shot our film entirely in the studio because of the light and the scenery and because there were so many exterior shots in it.

Lunching in the restaurant at Shepperton could be a surprising experience. At a neighboring table was what appeared to be a witch from a fairy story, and she was joined by a magician and by other characters who were obviously making a film about a fable. Then there appeared a giant—a real giant about seven feet tall, and broad and bulky in proportion, with a huge head, huge hands, wide leather belt, and big giant's boots. I had never seen a human being that big, but Kevin Kline said: "Oh, that's Andre, he does a lot of acting and he's also a famous wrestler."

I stole another look at where the giant was sitting, on a specially large chair, then saw the man next to him.

"Kevin," I said. "There's Meathead! You know, Archie Bunker's son-in-law! The one Archie's always being nasty to!"

Kevin looked around and he and Meathead waved to each other, then got up to exchange greetings. Kevin explained that Meathead, whose real name was Rob Reiner, was directing the film the giant and the other characters were in. It was called *The Princess Bride*, based on a William Goldman novel, and was shooting on a stage near the one we were using.

Before we finished with the township street set we had some appropriate visitors to the studio. First came John and Janet Marqusee, who as Paddington Press had published *Biko*; then we had John and Sheila Bush, formerly of Gollancz, who had published *Asking for Trouble*; and finally Michael Stern, who had first put the idea of our film project into Attenborough's head.

We also had visitors from Universal, including Sid Sheinberg, president of the parent company of Universal, MCA Inc., who were very excited by the assembly of rushes Attenborough showed them. In fact, Sid Sheinberg was so enthusiastic that Attenborough's smile reached the dimensions of dazzling friendliness so well described years earlier by William Goldman in his account of the Attenborough directorial style.

The theater for viewing rushes at Shepperton was a far cry from the old storeroom with the eggbox soundproofing we had used in Harare. Here were comfortable armchair-type seats, a big screen, and good sound quality.

The scene reenacting my first meeting with Steve Biko was shot in the replica of Biko's office on one of the Shepperton stages. It was a crucial scene in establishing the theme of the film, in introducing Denzel Washington to the audience as Biko, and in conveying the tensions between us at that first meeting. It was important to me that this tension should be conveyed because it seemed to me that whites in Africa, and white people all over the world who were not in sympathy with the Third World, all made the mistake I had made and had the same misconceptions I had had before meeting Steve Biko.

That mistake, that misconception, had been to evaluate black concerns from a white perspective—to view the Third World through the eyes of the First World.

Whites, and especially Anglo-Saxon whites, have no experience of group oppression. We don't know what it is like to be looked down on by anyone. We are part of the biggest in-group in the world, and while we may condemn racism and anti-Semitism we have no knowledge in our guts, in our very being, of what it is to be black in an antiblack environment or Jewish in an anti-Jewish environment.

I had gone to meet Biko as an adversary. I had condemned his Black Consciousness Movement as extreme, as antiwhite, as an overreaction to apartheid. I had gone partly out of interest. He had been described to me, by several whites who had met him, as highly intelligent.

If the film had projected him as immediately charming, and our first meeting as immediately friendly, it would have failed to convey the truth and the insight that I thought would be of most value to the audience. It was his uncompromising attitude that was important to convey—a rather scary attitude to someone tending to view issues from a unilateral attitude of certainty.

What Steve Biko taught me most was not the justice of the black cause—that was self-evident—but the fact that black people didn't have to conform to white criteria in their resistance to apartheid; didn't have to justify being black and holding a specifically black viewpoint of their situation. They did not have to enter my white terms of reference. While white sympathizers could be friends and even welcome allies in the campaign for liberation, they could not experience complete solidarity with blacks because they had not had the black experience.

To describe this attitude as racism was, I soon found out, a shallow judgment, and it seemed to me that the film could not convey this if it failed initially to convey the tensions at my first meeting with Steve Biko. Fortunately the scripted scene, and the way Attenborough shot it, reflected these concerns, which to my mind heightened the point of the friendship which later developed between Biko and me. I thought Kevin Kline conveyed the right amount of tentative irritation, and Denzel Washington the right degree of hardness without being objectionable. The "chemistry" between the two actors felt right to me.

After this scene we moved onto the big soundstage containing the duplication of our Ridge Road house set, for scenes involving our family and in particular the reenactment of the incident in which our five-year-old daughter, Mary, had been sent a T-shirt saturated with acid-based powder by the Security Police.

This happened after the death of Steve Biko. The local Security Police, resenting my articles and speeches on the Biko killing, intercepted a parcel containing two tiny T-shirts which could only have fitted a very small child. The T-shirts had the face of Steve Biko on the front and had been sent by Biko supporters.

Warrant Officers Marais and Van Schalkwyk were seen by postal staff collecting this parcel to take it to the Security Police offices for vetting before we could be allowed to receive it. At the Security Police office, a black cleaner saw them examining the T-shirts, then spraying them with what was later analyzed to be a substance called ninhydrin, before replacing them in the parcel and clearing it for delivery to us.

Ninhydrin produced a burning sensation. I handled the T-shirt after we had got it off Mary, and my hands stung for a long time after even that brief contact. It also turned the skin a violet color. Fortunately the efforts were not long-lasting, and after treatment Mary recovered within several hours; the discoloration was gone two days later.

But when she had opened the parcel, seen that the small T-shirt was for her, and put it on, she had screamed in agony within seconds.

After our escape I went to New Scotland Yard in London and then to police headquarters in Gothenburg, Sweden, to investigate the nature and origin of ninhydrin. It had been invented in Sweden in connection with a celebrated case called "the Helander case," in which a man who wanted to be bishop of Uppsala had sent anonymous typed letters urging his own election. Swedish chemists had produced the acid-based substance, which reacted to amino acids in the skin, so that if you had touched a piece of paper your fingertips could be discerned by applying ninhydrin to the paper, even a long time after you had touched it. The fingerprints showed up in livid purple or violet color. The Swedish chief of police in Gothenburg had arranged a demonstration for me as he explained the background to the invention of the substance, and I noticed that even the bottle it was in had been handled

141

with rubber gloves. As a rule, he said, ninhydrin was supplied only to police forces.

On the day of the T-shirt attack on Mary, I knew for the first time what it felt like to want to kill people. For several days the feeling persisted strongly, until it was clear that the physical effects of the ninhydrin were not permanent. I had in the house two lethal weapons— one an immensely powerful riot gun—and if I had had the slightest pretext for using it on Warrant Officers Marais and Van Schalkwyk during those few days before Mary was fully recovered, I wouldn't have had the least hesitation. In fact, I fervently wished for the opportunity. I hoped they would be lurking around the house at night so that I could say I had thought they were burglars. I would have blasted them.

Mary had been excited on receiving the parcel and had torn it open and eagerly pulled the T-shirt over her head. When she began screaming we couldn't work out the reason. "It's burning! My eyes are burning!" was all we could get out of her. Then we began to see the inflammation of the skin on her face, neck, and shoulders, and rang the doctor as we tried to sponge off whatever was burning her.

Our friend Donald Card, an ex-policeman, gathered evidence and statements implicating Marais and Van Schalkwyk, but the police investigating it took it no further. A young officer who seemed serious about the investigation was taken off the case, and no prosecution was ever instituted. Speaking in the South African Parliament, Police Minister Kruger announced that his department had evidence that I had engineered the whole incident myself, in order to discredit the Security Police.

Attenborough had worried for weeks about how he would shoot the T-shirt scene. He would look at little Spring Stuart-Walker, who was playing Mary, and say: "Somehow I'm going to have to get that kid to scream in agony!" But when the day came to shoot the scene, his long private talk with Spring and her own acting ability resulted in a convincing scream, and every appearance of agony, in four successive takes. After each call of "Cut!" she'd turn off the agony and giggle amusedly.

Again I was impressed at the makeup artistry of Wally Schneiderman and Beryl Lerman. They never overstated the horror of the marks on

142

Mary, and in fact understated them slightly—for the by-now familiar reason that an absolutely accurate depiction of what Mary had looked like that day would have led audiences to believe there had been exaggeration.

When the scene was finished Attenborough presented Spring with a number of beautifully packaged presents—mainly dolls, which she loved—and everyone applauded. She had earned the regard of the hardened professionals as well as the not-so-hardened ones.

The children were also needed for the shots of the interior of the aircraft flying from Maseru, Lesotho, to Botswana. For film purposes the plane had taken off at Charles Prince Airport, Harare, representing Maseru airport, and now here it was flying inside a closed studio at Shepperton.

Well, not really flying, of course. It was the torso of a plane mounted on a platform about ten feet high against a backdrop of painted cloud formations; the platform was being gently rocked by David Tomblin and his men to simulate the movement of a small plane flying through clouds. To boost the cloud illusion someone stood firing bursts from a sort of fire extinguisher past the plane windows, so that it looked like fresh, moving, close-in cloud.

Inside the plane the camera filmed Kevin Kline, Penelope Wilton, the children, Nicholas Tate (playing the pilot), and Louis Mahoney.

Louis Mahoney played the Lesotho government official who flew with me and my family from Lesotho to Botswana after the South African government had threatened to force the plane down. The Lesotho official, John Monyane, was later appointed to the Lesotho High Commission in Canada, and we had a reunion lunch in Ottawa six years later.

At the lunch I said to John: "My family and I were so impressed with you that day. There we were, flying more than two hours with the fear that the plane might be intercepted, and all you did all the time was read a book!"

He replied: "What none of you realized was that I was on the same page for two hours!"

The pilot Nick Tate was playing was a New Zealander, Richie de Montauk, who was a man of few words but had been determined to fly us out to safety. During that nerve-racking flight I asked Richie:

"What if they send jets to force us down?" He answered: "I'll go down to five hundred feet and see what those jets can do down there!"

I was reassured by this reply, only to learn after our landing in Botswana that Richie had merely been comforting me, because apparently jets could do practically anything that low—certainly as much as, and more than, a propeller-driven Britten-Norman Islander!

Next we filmed the interior shots of the deputy high commissioner's office. While waiting for the lighting to be arranged and the camera to be set up, Alec McCowen asked me what Jim Moffatt had really said once the official part of granting me asylum was completed.

I told him it had been: "Gave the bastards the slip, did you!"

During the shooting of this scene I suffered a mental aberration. I noticed that Kevin Kline had his (my) glasses back on; I stepped forward, interrupting the proceedings, to point this out. Eveyone looked at me strangely. Then I realized that the continuity was quite right—that having got across the border I had no longer been in disguise and had put my glasses back on, so Kevin was correctly bespectacled. I was comprehensively hooted by everyone for this strange lapse, not least by Attenborough.

Then we moved to Sandown Racetrack to turn it into Johannesburg airport for the scene of my arrest and banning. Stuart Craig and his cohorts had again produced total deception. I practically expected to hear the "stewardesses" speaking Afrikaans. This was again a weird reliving in exact detail of an exact occurrence of nine years before, even to the way the Security Police had waited until Bruce Haigh had said good-bye and I had walked through to the passport desk.

On that day Bruce had driven me to the airport. It was October 19, 1977, and from early morning there had been reports that critics of the government were being arrested and detained or banned. I hadn't expected to be among them, not being radical in the sense that some of the first to be arrested were. But as the day wore on the Security Police had started arresting nonradical critics as well. Shortly after lunch I had been in the office of the Reverend Beyers Naude, director of the Christian Institute, where with Cedric Mayson we had joked about being "on the list."

By the time Bruce started to drive me to the airport both Beyers and Cedric had been arrested and banned, and Bruce thought the

Security Police might be waiting for me at the airport. I thought it possible but unlikely, as I was not in the same political league as Beyers and Cedric in terms of importance.

When we arrived at the airport Bruce insisted on waiting with me until my flight was called. I waved good-bye to him and walked through to passport control, to find the Security Police officers waiting around the corner for me.

Kevin Kline and John Hargreaves accurately reenacted our dialogue and actions in the airport scene, causing me to grow angry all over again at the banning. But only for a moment, as I realized, just as after a bad dream, that this was now safe old England in as prosaic a setting as Sandown racecourse.

(Seven years after our banning I had a reunion with Beyers Naude, then unbanned and visiting New York, and we laughed over the events of that day. I recalled how, as I had left his office, I had asked for his clerical blessing to ward off arrest and banning, and he had administered it. I reminded him of this, adding: "Your blessing wasn't so bloody hot, was it?" and he nodded, laughing even harder.)

The last full scene to be shot was the scene of Kevin Kline in the black Valiant car with his two Security Police captors who had intercepted him at the airport. This time the Valiant was also up on a platform being given the rocking treatment while a huge drum behind displayed what looked like passing scenery by night and someone in front of the Valiant made swooping gestures with a strong light to represent passing cars.

On the last day, four months to the day since we had started filming at Ridge Road in Harare, we did assorted odds and ends. For the last camera setup Attenborough called me up to "direct," so that at last I got a chance to say: "Action!"—though I botched the timing of the first call through excitement. Then to general merriment Attenborough punched me in the ribs for imitating his stance and calling: "Action, darlings!"

Then came the final call: "Cut!"

And it was all over.

The shooting, that is. The professionals hastened to say that, in the broader sense, the film was only half made at this stage, as there would be six months of cutting, editing, music, dubbing, mixing, and finally titling. But the shooting was over. We had another "wrap party," and the pleasure of completing the schedule was tempered only by the sadness of parting from so many of the unit who would now go on to other films, or on well-deserved vacation.

But I already had the feeling that Attenborough had shot an unusually good film; that he had taken a good script and, in my view, shot "above it"—made the most of it aesthetically and artistically. I also thought it would be good because, as objectively as I could judge, it was an interesting and true story portrayed by excellent actors.

From now on the center of operations was to be Twickenham Studios.

With the shooting completed and the editing well advanced, I went to Los Angeles and spent a week at Universal Studios to get to know something of the organization backing and distributing our film. In particular I was interested to find out why Universal, the biggest and reputedly the most profit-oriented of the major studios, was to become the first to release a feature film tackling the controversial subject of apartheid.

My first surprise was the atmosphere at Universal. I had expected to find an impersonal air about the place such as one encounters on walking unannounced into most mammoth organizations, but my initial impressions were of smiling faces, and they weren't smiling at me— they were smiling at each other and into telephones.

I had made an appointment to see Brian Lindquist of the publicity department, and being used to British ways I had arranged it for around noon. Few British executives in the corporate world of the City of London get into what they regard as their stride before ten A.M.; on learning that Mr. Lindquist and his colleagues began their working day at 7:30 I suddenly recalled that I was now in America. One of his associates, Alan Sutton, actually got up by the dawn's early light to jog before driving for more than an hour up the San Diego Freeway to get to work at this time; I preferred not to think about what time he had to get out of bed to fit all this in.

Another early impression at Universal was of youth. Not only Brian Lindquist and Alan Sutton but all the executives I met were considerably younger than I expected them to be—including the chairman,

Tom Pollock, the president of production, Sean Daniel, and the president of marketing, Ed Roginski, though when I researched the biographies of the latter three it became clear that, though young in years, they were old in experience of the motion-picture industry. They had, as the Americans say, been around.

Tom Pollock and Sean Daniel had returned the day before from London, where Attenborough had shown them an advanced rough cut of the film, and they were highly enthusiastic about it. Ed Roginski was already considering marketing projections based on the idea of a year-end release, which meant maximum promotion aimed at the optimum cinema-attendance period.

Attenborough had told me that Ed Roginski was preeminent in his field, arguably the number one film marketing man in the world. He had been hugely impressed by Roginski's handling of the *Gandhi* marketing when he had been with Columbia, and was confident that we couldn't be in better hands for the marketing of *Cry Freedom*.

Politically this was good news to me, because the more people who saw the film the more public opinion in the West would provoke strong international action to end apartheid. In terms of impact the film seemed to have everything going for it—the political sensitivity and cinematic art of Attenborough and his British team, and the American know-how and promotional resources that would be unleashed by Universal to get the film to the largest number of people.

This meant that Diana Hawkins as director of publicity would have the same scale and caliber of support and would be working with the same top team she had enjoyed working with on *Gandhi*. I thought now for the thousandth time how much our film owed that brilliant South African lawyer who had returned to his country of birth to lead the great Indian nation along the path to independence.

Word of the favorable impact of the rough cut had spread rapidly through the legendary "black tower," the headquarters building at Universal City of the parent company, MCA Inc., headed by Lew Wasserman as chairman and Sid Sheinberg, who had visited the set at Shepperton during the closing stages of shooting, as president. Good reports of the rough cut had certainly percolated down to the efficient young woman in the publicity department who organized transport for me whenever I needed it.

Her name, I first thought, was Donette Brown, but after a while I came to realize that her first name was Dawnette. There are subtleties about the "aw" sound in American pronunciation which can be misleading to non-Americans. In my book *Biko* I had explained that the name was pronounced "Bee-kaw," not realizing that Americans pronounced *aw* as "ah." I should have said that the last syllable rhymed with "floor" but without the "r" sound.

There are other transatlantic pitfalls of pronunciation. On my first visit to the United States I had labored for several days under the illusion that a certain lady's name was Paddy, only to discover that it was Patti, and that a man I had heard described as a rider was actually a writer.

Anyway, thanks to the help of Brian Lindquist, Alan Sutton, and Dawnette Brown, I was able to snoop around at will through Universal City and wander through the large complex of buildings surrounding the "black tower." The whole area had once been a chicken ranch until its purchase in 1915 by an enterprising immigrant from Bavaria named Carl Laemmle. Laemmle, who founded the Universal Film Company in 1912, paid $165,000 for the 230-acre ranch, which later expanded into 420 acres worth today more than the gross national product of half the countries of the world. California alone, it has been noted, would if separate and independent be the seventh wealthiest country in the world.

The popular belief is that Los Angeles became the film capital of the world because of its sunny climate, but more important reasons were cheap nonunion labor and the area's distance from the East Coast tentacles of the Mob. Gangsters on the East Coast had such a firm grip on the film distribution business in the early days of silent film there that many filmmakers headed for the furthest geographic point from New Jersey—Los Angeles. It was before the age of commercial flight, and, as it took three days by train from coast to coast, the producers were able to release and patent their films before the East Coast gangsters could pirate them.

Laemmle was an interesting blend of daring and caution. He was daring enough to start a film studio in what was then a rural area used for chicken ranching, yet cautious enough to keep the hens and sell the eggs until the studio was turning a profit.

The first picture completed at Universal was *Damon and Pythias* and the first lady among the stars at Universal in those days was the improbably named Florence Lawrence, billed as Queen of the Screen. Universal's first talkie was *Showboat*, whose assistant director, Jack Foley, was so good at contriving noises to dub into the soundtrack that the phrase "to Foley it" is still used in America to describe the reproduction of synthesized sound effects.

It was at Universal that the best-known horror films were pioneered, with Boris Karloff, Lon Chaney, and Bela Lugosi, as well as the best of the early science-fiction films and westerns starring Tom Mix, Buck Jones, and Tex Ritter. I was especially interested to learn that it was at Universal that the twelve famous Sherlock Holmes films were made, and that those foggy London streets had been created at the former chicken ranch rather than in England as I had supposed. Universal had therefore been instrumental in boosting the career of the South African actor Basil Rathbone, as Holmes, as they later did for another already-recognized South African actress, Juliet Prowse, in the musical *Sweet Charity*.

Another South African link with Hollywood was the man who captained England's first touring cricket team to South Africa in his younger days, C. Aubrey Smith, noted for his ability to deliver fast left-arm inswingers which swerved viciously in at the batsman's body. In later years, as Sir C. Aubrey Smith, he established the Hollywood cricket club, where Boris Karloff became known for the power of his coverdrive and David Niven bowled erratic legspin.

Comedy was also part of the Universal staple, featuring W. C. Fields, Bud Abbott and Lou Costello, and a long line of comedians including Steve Martin, Carol Burnett, and Dan Aykroyd of the modern era. It was also the studio which released most of the major Alfred Hitchcock films, and was now host to the modern master of the spectacular, Steven Spielberg, whose *E.T.* had become the most profitable film of all time, eclipsing even his phenomenally successful Universal release *Jaws*.

Walking around Universal City considering these facts, I thought that with Attenborough editing away in London and this lot firmly behind his endeavors financially and promotionally, Wendy and I were suddenly in heavyweight cinematic company. I thought back to the day in 1962 when we, young and newlywed, had come as tourists to

Los Angeles and had gone on the Universal tour. If anyone had told us then that this huge studio would one day release a major film including actual events in our lives and the lives of our future children, we would have backed away at such crazy talk and looked about for his keeper.

I decided to see how the Universal tour had progressed over the past twenty years.

Predictably, it had developed almost beyond recognition in its major elements, and was now offering features and effects as remarkable as any to be found at Disneyland. I found myself successively involved in a galactic laser-beam battle from which I was rescued by well-equipped earthlings; terrified by a giant animated King Kong who loomed considerably too close for insouciance; menaced by "Jaws" which emerged abruptly from a peaceful lake; rescued from a flash flood; and otherwise amused, scared, and entertained by one of the best shows on earth. It was not at all surprising to learn that the Universal tour had attracted more than fifty million tourists since its inception in 1964.

Before I left Universal I met several more executives who would be increasingly involved in the promotion, marketing, and distribution of our film. These included William Soady, Canadian-born president of the distribution division, Terry Nelson, vice president of production, who had visited us at Shepperton during the early screen tests, and Don Barrett, director of promotion; also Nadia Bronson, who would be working with Ed Roginski with particular responsibility for international promotion and marketing. As Diana Hawkins had put it: "Nadia's a Very Big Deal, very highly regarded."

Frank Price, the man who, as president of Universal, had initially backed *Cry Freedom*, was no longer with the company. I visited him at his home in Beverly Hills to ask why he had favored the idea from the beginning. A reserved but friendly man, he was like most Americans forthright in his replies to questions, including my question as to why he had left Universal. It had been said in a trade publication that the failure of a film about Howard the Duck was the reason, but while agreeing as a former journalist that the headline about a duck cooking his goose had been irresistible to the headline-writer, he said the real reason had been general policy differences.

As to his support for our film project, he said he had favored the idea of such a film even before joining Universal, when he had been head of Columbia. When Attenborough, with whom he had been associated through the distribution deal on *Gandhi*, had secured the option for the Biko story, it had seemed a good project to back.

Fortunately for us there had been general support at Universal for our project, so that when he had left the company his successors were equally enthusiastic and Attenborough was assured of the strength of their support throughout the production stage. Even more fortunately for us, their enthusiasm increased after they had seen the finished footage now approaching the "fine cut" stage in London.

A final point about Universal's backing for our project was that since the days of Carl Laemmle the studio had tended to favor, more than most major studios, films of international character. This was a general policy attitude reflecting the name Laemmle had chosen for the studio, and on going through the long list of Universal releases down the years I could see there was considerable support for this claim.

Back in London, the Universal office was headed by Ian Lewis, who had taken a keen interest in the shooting from an early stage, in fact as far back as the screen-testing, and who had visited us on location in Zimbabwe several times for liaison. Ian was friendly with Michael Williams-Jones, London-based head of United International Pictures, who would handle our film's international distribution. It had seemed a small world when, during a visit to the set at Shepperton, Michael Williams-Jones had told Wendy and me we three had something in common: he was from our hometown, East London, South Africa! In fact, his father had been our vet, and had treated our dog Charlie on several occasions . . .

The rough cut of a film, I learned, is the stage when the editor has assembled all the shot footage in sequence and has snipped out all the parts obviously to be dispensed with. But a lot of editing precedes this stage, and I asked Attenborough's editor, Lesley Walker, about her general approach to film editing.

She agreed with the jigsaw-puzzle analogy, which she thought ironic in view of her dislike of jigsaw puzzles as a child. "I used to hate them—I'd get to the sky part and think forget it, and put it back in the box." But with the puzzle of thousands of sections of film it was different. "I have a strange mind," she said. "No memory for names, addresses, or phone numbers—but if someone lays out a scene for me on film and there's a shot missing I may not know what the shot entails but I can remember from the rushes that there's a shot missing."

She said it was only when working with film that she felt decisive. Generally she didn't like making decisions, such as where to go on an outing, or what to wear. "I think that's why I wear black or dark blue all the time—then I don't have to make the decision in the morning. But with film it's the other way around."

Since her first job as film editor, on *Portrait of the Artist as a Young Man* in 1977, she had edited nine major productions, the most recent being *Letter to Brezhnev* and *Mona Lisa*. Assisted by Jeremy Hume, Lesley had pre-edited all the available sequences as shooting had progressed in Zimbabwe. When I saw how she achieved added impact by juxtaposing certain shots and sequences, it became clear how creative the editing process on a film could be.

When shooting was completed, her collaboration with Attenborough had intensified as he turned his full attention to the evolution of successive stages of the rough cut. Each successive assembly took on more and more impact; Wendy and I watched the whole thing tighten up to acquire greater pace and depth.

A shot of a look here, the change of an angle there, made all the difference to a scene, and we thought they added considerable force to the narrative by taking some scenes previously envisaged as flashbacks and putting them in chronological sequence instead, such as the main Biko courtroom scene and the Biko funeral.

The final phases of editing as we approached the "fine cut"—the film's ultimate visual form—reminded us of those machines that take paper and pulp and compact them into hardboard. In cinematic terms this meant that Attenborough and Lesley Walker had considered the significance of literally every foot of film shot and every second of projection time so that what finally appeared on the screen would be the best distillation from all the footage shot during the four months of production. Yet even this was far from the end of the postproduction process, because what we had now was the final form of the film visually. All the sound, including the music, now had to be added.

Much of the sound had of course already been recorded by Simon Kaye and his colleagues, during shooting on location and in the studio, but inevitably certain lines of dialogue weren't as clear as they had to be, and certain sounds—doors closing, footsteps, car engines—weren't of perfect quality in terms of consistency throughout all the sequences.

This, the next stage of postproduction, was the responsibility of Jonathan Bates, the supervising sound editor. Jonathan had begun his part of the process while we were on location in Zimbabwe, recording background noises typical of Southern Africa such as night noises and sounds of garden insects and birds. By the time we joined his sphere of operations it was March 1987 and he was recording particular sound effects at Twickenham Film Studios, where the production unit had moved for the final phases of editing and recording.

Our sound synchronization room had only recently been completed as part of a modernization scheme at Twickenham, and was now the most up-to-date in Europe, supplied with new computerized equipment. Here we did some revoicing with several members of the cast who had to repeat some of their lines in exact synchronization to their lip movements on the screen, usually because the recording on location had been spoiled by extraneous noise.

At one time, revoicing was achieved through a process called "looping." Sections of film for revoicing would be formed into loops going round and round on the projector, and the actors could respeak their lines over and over until their voices matched their lip movements perfectly. Now, however, there is a new process called Automated Dialogue Replacement in which the time-consuming looping of the film is no longer necessary. Computers make it possible to go back over sections of film repeatedly and to hear the playback immediately, so that precise timing can be achieved far more quickly.

We brought in London-based Xhosa-speaking South Africans to supply lines and background conversation where necessary, replacing the lines of the Shona-speaking extras in Zimbabwe, and Afrikaans-speaking whites to speak the police and army parts where appropriate.

Part of the sound studio had different sections of flooring—board, carpet, paving, and gravel—to simulate the appropriate surfaces in the film, and there were several types of door to be opened and closed for the right sound effect.

Jonathan Bates, son of the distinguished novelist H. E. Bates, had been one of Britain's top sound editors for thirty years, and had often worked on Attenborough films, so that he and Attenborough knew each other's ways well. In fact he had worked more often with Attenborough as director than had any other member of the crew.

He was resigned to frequent interruptions as Attenborough would be called to the phone, and knew that while he could proceed with his recording schedule the results would be closely scrutinized at the end of each call.

Attenborough's close involvement with all forms of postproduction was as marked in these closing stages as it had been in the beginning of the preproduction process, and nothing would induce him to let anything go by without his personal imprimatur.

Not even illness was permitted to interfere with his workaholism. For several days during January 1987 he had suffered an acute attack of diverticulitis—an agonizing condition in which severe abdominal pains come in cycles—and his assistant, Clare Howard, told Wendy and me that Attenborough's pain had been so great for a time that he had—while dictating letters to her—been literally down on his hands and knees, with perspiration pouring from his face.

"You mean he kept dictating letters through all this?" said Wendy.

"Well, yes, actually," said Clare. "In between spasms!"

Working closely with Jonathan was John Bateman, who operated the computerized console. In a manner mysterious to me, he could track down and replay any of an amazing number of recorded takes, splitting some up and joining together others to make different combinations of dialogue as required by Attenborough.

There was constant amused confusion arising from the similarities of name between Jon Bates and John Bateman, and Attenborough kidded them constantly about this. They in turn clearly enjoyed working with him in between his plate-twirls and were vastly amused when on one of the final days Attenborough briefly became a suitcase.

It happened like this. In the scene where the children crossed the bridge into Lesotho there was some revoicing needed of a shot where Adam Stuart-Walker, playing the part of Duncan, had to speak while carrying a heavy suitcase. To get Adam to simulate the strained voice of a child carrying a heavy case, Attenborough crouched down in front of him as he respoke the line, dragging down on his hands to create the weight of the suitcase.

One of the unit observed: "Now I've seen everything! Now Dickie's even played the role of a bloody suitcase!"

When Jonathan Bates had completed the sound synchronization process, the focal point of postproduction became the dubbing or sound-mixing theater—a large-screen studio with consoles that made it look like the flight deck of the starship *Enterprise*. This impressive flight deck was under the command of Gerry Humphreys, regarded by a number of directors, including Attenborough, as one of the real masters of the art of dubbing and mixing sound. Working closely with Gerry Humphreys was his son Dean, his longtime colleague in this special art.

It was quite an experience to enter this big and marvelously appointed theater of operations. Here all the sound was mixed together—dialogue, background noises, music, sound effects—with facilities for dozens of soundtracks to be consolidated onto a single track. Here there could be complete creative experimentation—trying out a sequence with certain sounds brought up in volume, or muted, in search of the best blend.

This was where the ultimate form of the film was finally determined through the addition of the totality of the sound to the totality of the visual work.

Central to the sound was, of course, the music.

During the years we had been living in Britain I had occasionally been struck by the beauty of certain bits of music on television and on the screen. I liked the orchestration and the approach to such music as the BBC news theme, and to the production *An Englishman Abroad*. It was only later that I learned the identity of the composer, who turned out to be the composer chosen by Attenborough to do the music for our film. Later when I saw his name on film scores I knew the music would be good.

Wendy and I first met George Fenton in a hot lunch tent on location in Zimbabwe. I was introduced to this apparently shy young man with very black hair who seemed diffidently attentive to what everyone else said to him but showed no readiness to do much talking himself. Later, when I got to know him a bit better, I found that George Fenton didn't at all mind talking when he felt it appropriate, and that what he had to say was as interesting as the man himself.

I am always in awe of composers, because composing music is one of the life careers I would choose if given the extra life and the necessary talent. (Then would come life as a professional chess player, cricketer, and tennis player, then maybe architect . . .)

Barely into his middle thirties, George Fenton already had so many credits for scores of major productions like *Gandhi* and *The Jewel in the Crown* that he must, I thought, have been one of those prodigies who grasp notation and counterpoint while in the cradle and write sonatas at the age of five.

But no. Though there had been some music in his family—both his parents played the piano a bit—he was eight before he wanted to learn an instrument, and that instrument was the guitar. He was taught by an odd-job man who came to the house as a chimney sweep. Then at school he started playing the organ, though he proved better with the feet than with the hands, finding the pedals easier to master than the keyboard. Feeling the lack of a truly good keyboard technique, he moved back to the guitar, and started playing with a band.

He had a go at acting, but felt he didn't measure up, then got a call from Carl Davis, with whom he had done an album when they both worked on the show *Forty Years On*. Davis was doing a show at the Aldwych and wanted George to play the guitar in it.

At this point it struck me that anyone who had done an album with Carl Davis and had been invited to play again had to be pretty damn good, and made a mental note that henceforth everything the modest Fenton said about his abilities had to be recognized as a massive understatement.

In 1974 a producer who thought George was someone else gave him a playing part in another show, and when one of the songs couldn't be found George wrote it himself, literally overnight. It was well received, and launched him on the road to bigger and better composing jobs. There followed years of learning this demanding craft, during which he felt he benefited by having to learn at what he calls "the sharp end"—motivated by fear of impending deadlines and critical orchestras.

"One of my fears was that an orchestra would look at what I'd written and say: 'This is no good—it won't work.' But of course they never do say that."

He said he panicked in the beginning, and still panicked now though for different reasons. "You go on panicking because you have more to lose."

He had only once played in a full orchestra before composing orchestral music, but again ascribed his plunge into this dimension of music to fear. "It tends to concentrate the mind," he says, but adds: "The privilege is being able to hear what you have written almost immediately. If you are at college, or studying composition with someone, it is very difficult to get someone to play your work, whereas in my situation I was hearing it played by the best. In film and television the quality of playing is very high. If you write something, an oboe solo or something like that, you get some simply brilliant player—he doesn't just play the notes, he plays everything you have ever dreamed it could sound like!"

Working closely with George Fenton on the music for *Cry Freedom* was an immensely talented musician named Jonas Gwangwa. Exiled from South Africa since 1960, he had been born into a musical family in Orlando township, near Johannesburg, where they'd had a piano at home. As a boy Jonas joined the Huddleston Jazz Band, a group formed by Father Trevor Huddleston, who as an Anglican archbishop was to become an international leader of the worldwide antiapartheid campaign. In this group Jonas got his first trombone, but as no one knew how to teach him to hold it he studied pictures of Glenn Miller to find out, and became so skilled on the instrument that he played with some of South Africa's best musicians, including Todd Matshikiza, Hugh Masekela, and Miriam Makeba, and toured abroad with the successful black musical *King Kong*.

In New York he attended the Manhattan School of Music, where

157

he studied for his degree in music, and played in a group backing Harry Belafonte and Miriam Makeba before forming his own group. Then he was appointed director of the Amandla Cultural Ensemble of the African National Congress, comprised largely of highly talented young musicians who had escaped into exile after the police crackdowns following the 1976 Soweto uprising. The best of these became the core of Amandla—about thirty who perform drama, dance, song, and poetry, and have a sixteen-piece band playing *Mbaqanga*, South African township jazz.

Jonas Gwangwa, now in his late forties, was introduced to Attenborough by Dali Tambo and readily agreed to work with George Fenton on the music for the film. They became a formidable combination, and when at the first recording session I heard the blend of George's brilliant orchestration and Jonas's typically South African harmonies and rhythms, my hair stood on end with excitement.

The orchestral augmentation of the anthem "Nkosi Sikelele iAfrika" with which *Cry Freedom* ends is an emotional tour de force, and I'll be surprised if even those audiences unfamiliar with African music remain unstirred by it.

Fortunately, George Fenton had the artistic generosity to welcome the collaboration of Jonas on the music, and was glad to do so on professional grounds. He didn't accommodate Jonas merely to please Attenborough, though his regard for Attenborough was so high that Fenton wouldn't lightly have disregarded such a suggestion. Having worked with Attenborough on *Gandhi*, he had become a confirmed admirer of Sir Richard, not only for his tenacity in getting the film made after twenty years of setbacks and delays, but because of his perspective during the scoring for the film.

"While working on the music for *Gandhi* I was having an awful problem with a particular part of it. I struggled with it every way and really what was psyching me out was that if someone had spent twenty years getting a film made what bar of music could possibly be great enough? It was a mind-blowing problem and I spent literally days sitting motionless by the piano. Finally I said to him that I felt all psyched out by it.

"And there was this person who had just finished shooting in India and had been backward and forward countless times over the last ten years and had sold pictures to raise the money, and he turned round to me and said: 'It's only a movie, darling.' That is really his integrity.

"He is tremendously courageous to do subjects on film about which he deeply cares. . . . He sets himself up to be criticized by various factions but he chooses that particular subject and that is very courageous, because there are a lot of safe things you could make films about."

EPILOGUE

L ooking back at the end of the film and at the end of this book, I remain moved by Attenborough's self-confidence, the courage displayed in making *Cry Freedom*. It was Steve Biko's courage that originally stirred me out of my comfortable and complacent rut of affluence in South Africa; later it was the courage of Ntsiki Biko and Steve's political associates reinforced by the heroism of black South Africans generally in fighting with few weapons—mostly spiritual— against a deadly white armory.

Then there was the courage of members of my own family, each of whom at various times and in various ways impressed me deeply with their respective strengths. Wendy has always had an often disconcertingly honest directness of approach to moral issues that leads by the shortest route to confrontation. From the time we first came into conflict with our fellow whites in South Africa, and ultimately with our government, she was always ready to support any fight against them which she felt was justified—particularly the final fight over the killing of Steve Biko. Her political judgment had become invaluable to me since soon after we were married, and over the years this extended to her literary judgment as well; but throughout our time in South Africa and through many conflicts and confrontations at various times with my employers, with local government officials, and ultimately with the national government, it was her spirit and strength that carried the day.

Her courage became even more remarkable in exile, when in circumstances and against odds that would have destroyed a weaker person she began a new career, accepting speaking engagements and writing for major newspapers while rebuilding a firm base for the family six thousand miles from home.

Postproduction work on *Cry Freedom* was completed shortly before our twenty-fifth wedding anniversary, and I felt lucky indeed to have shared a quarter-century with the person whose thoughts, feelings, and opinions mattered more to me than those of any other human being.

As for the children, each in turn showed such character under disruption and stress that I still marvel at it. Jane, who as the eldest had to make the hardest leap from one educational system to another, managed to graduate from university with a good degree. Mary, who could have been expected to suffer lifelong trauma resulting from the T-shirt incident, has proved the happiest and best-balanced teenager imaginable. To have gone through our trials of readjustment without her sunny personality at home would have been much harder. Dillon, Duncan, and Gavin went at various times through periods and patterns of behavior that made us wonder if they would adjust successfully to their new environment, yet each in a special way showed unforeseen strength of character under challenge. Dillon developed such a rocklike dependability in some respects that there is no one I could more confidently entrust with a specific mission of importance. Duncan and Gavin manifested markedly different though impressive achievements of their own as well, and all three boys came through harrowing times and changes in their lifestyle more bravely than I think I could have managed at their age.

There are many kinds of courage. The courage of a Steve Biko is heroic. The courage of children uprooted from their homes is stoic.

Then there is that far more subtle and often more complex courage—moral courage, such as the courage of a member of the British Establishment stepping constantly out of the hallowed bounds of that Establishment to expose the most controversial evils—and, what is more, to succeed.

There is an element in British society which deeply resents success and mercilessly hounds the successful. So far, Attenborough has confounded advocates of this position. He has managed to retain a broad popularity in Britain in spite of his success, and in fact generally his countrymen are proud of his achievements in many fields. But let him stumble badly once, and it may be a different story—especially if the task chosen is a controversial one. And that is why his attitude is courageous. Instead of resting on his laurels and basking in the approval of his peers, he dares again and again to "press the envelope" and walk the tightrope. And he is a doer, not a presider. Almost to the point of obsession, he is totally involved in each of his many projects—in the front line with his sleeves rolled up, as with this film. When I look back over the years of preproduction, production, and postproduction of this film, virtually no element of the venture comes to mind separate from the image of his total participation at every stage. During the shaping of the script; during the screen-testing and casting; during the production design, the location scouting, the shooting, the editing, the sound recording, the dubbing, and finally the scoring and titling, Attenborough was central to every phase and every part of every phase.

This is truly his film, and to call him merely producer and director seems inadequate.

Nobody else I know could have done it. The many months of diplomacy required in dealing with the various factions in the South African liberation struggle; the reserves of energy required to deal with obstacle after obstacle; the cruel accusations, destructive attacks, and campaign of damaging lies he had to put up with from certain quarters in South Africa; the physical strength and mental stamina needed to initiate, supervise, and complete *Cry Freedom*—these manifold demands were of a scale and intensity few human beings could have coped with and withstood.

At times I was reminded of those traction toys which churn along the floor. You can lift them and move them back the whole length of the room, and they immediately churn on as if nothing had happened. Attenborough was like that after every setback. He immediately churned on, wasting no time in realigning himself. He had at all times what Wendy calls a "sure center"—a confident sense of who he was and what he was about, existing independently of anyone else and therefore impervious to distraction from his goals. It was a phrase often applied to Steve Biko by those who knew him.

With the film complete, I think back also to the unsung heroes of the unit—the many people who got things done, as professionally and thoroughly as the leading personalities involved. I think particularly of people like Cordelia Donohoe, a junior member of the second unit on location, who through long boiling days in the sun at Bulawayo and Harare was literally on the run from morning until night. I remember being touched to see so much energy and dedication by someone who had never met Steve Biko or his fellow victims of apartheid but was giving the job all she had because she believed in our film and in what it could achieve.

It was a privilege to be associated with such people. Seeing the final result on the screen has confirmed my belief that *Cry Freedom* will succeed in raising the awareness of many millions all over the world as to the iniquity of apartheid, and will move many of them to demand of their political representatives and their governments that more must be done by the international community to help bring this crime against humanity to an end.